THE
FINANCIAL SECTOR
OF THE AMERICAN
ECONOMY

edited by
STUART BRUCHEY
University of Maine

A GARLAND SERIES

BANK FAILURES
AND DEREGULATION
IN THE 1980s

LINDA M. HOOKS

GARLAND PUBLISHING, Inc.
NEW YORK & LONDON / 1994

Library of Congress Cataloging-in-Publication Data

Hooks, Linda M., 1962–
     Bank failures and deregulation in the 1980s / Linda M. Hooks.
        p.   cm. — (The Financial sector of the American economy)
     Includes bibliographical references and index.
     ISBN 0–8153–1739–5
     1. Banks and banking—United States—History.   2. Bank failures—
United States—History.   3. Banks and banking—United States—
Deregulation.   4. Banks and banking—United States—State supervision.
5. Deposit insurance—United States.   6. Banks and banking—
Louisiana—Deregulation—Case studies.   I. Title. II. Series.
HG2491.H65   1994
332.1'0973'09048—dc20   94-485
                                                                              CIP

Printed on acid-free, 250-year-life paper
Manufactured in the United States of America

To my parents

Contents

Acknowledgments

For their many helpful discussions, I wish to recognize my dissertation committee members: Trudy Cameron, Bill Gale, Axel Leijonhufvud, Eric Rasmusen, Siew Hong Teoh, and Michael Waldman. I especially thank Professor Leijonhufvud, for introducing me to many fascinating issues in monetary economics; Professor Waldman, for guiding me through the formation of the theoretical model and for devoting generous amounts of time to my dissertation; and Professor Cameron, for advising me on all aspects of the empirical work.

Thanks to Jane Murdoch, Graeme Woodbridge, Nancy Cole, and Barry Freeman, for offering critical comments, advice on technical matters, and moral support; and to Tim Opler, for assistance in obtaining CRSP data. Thanks to my parents, my sister, and my family for their continuing support.

Illustrations

Tables

Bank Failures
and Deregulation
in the 1980s

I. Introduction

Signs of financial distress are numerous in the U.S. economy today. Bank failures are at record levels, the funds of the Federal Deposit Insurance Corporation are under stress from its efforts to close insolvent banks, and the question of the government's role in these financial problems has become a highly-publicized political debate.

The issue of financial stability has occupied an important place in economic discussion for years; intertwined with this issue is the problem of the appropriate role of government in the financial structure. Advocates of a free banking system, for example, White [1984], hold that government intervention is neither necessary nor desirable; while adherents of the view that the financial system is not stable, like Kindleberger [1989], believe that government intervention is needed. Measures designed to avert or lessen financial crises usually involve regulation, deposit insurance, and the designation of a lender of last resort. When crises occur in spite of these policies, the effectiveness of the policies is questioned.

This book explores the relationship between financial stability and institutional structure by examining the connection between bank risk-taking and institutional changes caused by deregulation. Two important features of the U.S. banking system will be highlighted: the presence of fixed-rate deposit insurance, and government regulation of banks. Kareken [1981, 1983] proposes that, while this type of deposit insurance encourages banks to choose riskier investments than is optimal, the distortion may be controlled by government regulation of banks. Thus, deregulation allows greater risk-taking by banks and may be a contributing factor in the present wave of bank failures.

The impact of deregulation on bank risk-taking is tested on data from individual Louisiana banks for the period 1974-89. A measure of bank riskiness, a pseudo-beta derived from the capital asset pricing model, is employed to explore changes in bank risk-taking over the sample period. This measure should more accurately quantify systematic risk than measures used in previous studies because it captures the

3

interdependence of returns on the different assets in a bank's portfolio. Two additional measures of risk, a pseudo-variance and the discrete outcome of survival or failure of a bank, capture the total riskiness of a bank. The relationship between these risk measures and deregulation of deposit interest rates is then tested.

Tests using the pseudo-beta measure of risk demonstrate that deposit interest rates have a significant positive effect on risk in the post-deregulation period; in the pre-deregulation period the relationship is negative.   When tests use measures of total risk, a positive relationship continues to hold for the post-deregulation period. Two alternate specifications of the empirical model, a fixed-effects model and a simultaneous-equations model, corroborate the results of the basic model. Additionally, a two-stage failure model incorporates this interest rate-risk relationship into a probability-of-bank-failure model. Estimates of this model show that interest-rate deregulation increases the probability of bank failure.

The remainder of this book is organized as follows: Chapter II provides an overview of the U.S. and Louisiana banking systems. Chapter III chronicles the Louisiana economy over the years in the data set. In Chapter IV, previous theoretical and empirical works related to financial stability are summarized. Chapter V formulates a simple model which demonstrates the link between deposit interest rates and bank portfolio riskiness. The data set of Louisiana banks and the construction of a new measure of bank riskiness are described in Chapter VI. Chapter VII formulates and tests the basic empirical model; an extension of this model, the two-stage failure model, comprises the Chapter VIII. A final chapter summarizes the evidence presented and explores the resultant policy implications.

II. Institutional Features of the U.S. Financial System

    The U.S. financial system experienced rapid and significant changes in the past decade. At the same time, bank failures climbed to levels not seen since the 1930's. This section offers a brief history of the U.S. and Louisiana banking systems over the past sixty years, necessary to place the recent institutional changes and bank failures in proper perspective. Relevant institutions examined include the Federal Deposit Insurance Corporation (FDIC), federal government regulations for banks, and state regulations specific to the banks in the data set. These institutional features have been blamed, in various combinations, for the record number of bank failures, and so have been the targets of calls for reform. The assorted viewpoints regarding causes of current problems and possible reforms are reviewed in the concluding paragraphs of this chapter.

    While much attention has been devoted to the savings and loan failures across the U.S., a similar wave of bank failures has developed that has received somewhat less attention. In 1985, bank failures in the U.S. reached a record high level, and have surpassed that record in each year since. This phenomenon is illustrated in Figure 1, which presents bank failures in the U.S., as a percentage of all insured banks, for each year since the founding of the FDIC in 1933; and Figure 2, which shows failures in Louisiana, as a percentage of all insured Louisiana banks, for the same period. The rise in failures in the 1980's in both figures is pronounced. Figure 3 and Figure 4 chart the same bank failures weighted by their relative deposit size in the U.S. and Louisiana. As shown in these figures, the magnitude of the failures in the 1980's is substantial; in 1989, almost two percent of all U.S. banks, holding over one percent of total U.S. deposits, failed during the year. Explanations of this considerable increase in bank failures usually place primary blame on deteriorating local economic conditions. However, the increase in failures also generally coincides with the deregulation of the

5

banking system described below. It is the significance of this relationship that is empirically explored in this book.

The federal government regulates banks in two ways: through direct legislative actions and through oversight by several government agencies. The basic structure of the U.S. banking system is formed from legislation passed in the early part of the century that imposed strict regulations on bank activities. One important piece of such legislation is the Banking Act of 1933, which initiated regulation of deposit interest rates and restrictions on the assets that banks may hold. More recently, the U.S. Congress reversed its objective, choosing deregulation of bank activities as the new goal. In 1980, Congress passed the Depository Institution Deregulation and Monetary Control Act (DIDMCA), which repealed most ceilings on interest rates paid on deposits. The 1980 Act also required all banks to hold reserves with a Federal Reserve Bank, and raised Federal Deposit Insurance Corporation (FDIC) insurance coverage to $100,000. Finally, in 1982, the Garn-St. Germain Act significantly deregulated the savings and loan industry; this, too, may have had some indirect effects on banks through competition between banks and savings and loans.

Another relevant institution introduced by the U.S. Congress is the Federal Deposit Insurance Corporation, established in 1933 in part to prevent widespread bank failures. A run on a single insolvent bank could spread to other banks as public confidence in the banking system wavered. In order to prevent the contagion of bank runs and instill public confidence in the banking system, Congress created the FDIC, which guaranteed protection from losses on deposits at insured banks. The original limit of $5,000 per account on insurance coverage has been increased several times, and was raised in the 1980 DIDMCA, as noted above, to the present $100,000. In practice, deposit insurance coverage has been unlimited; this is due to the FDIC method of closing failed banks. The FDIC usually closes banks through a "purchase and assumption" agreement (P and A) with a healthy bank or banks. In essence, this means that the FDIC offers assistance to a healthy bank in purchasing a failed bank, so that all deposits are transferred to the healthy bank. In a purchase and assumption transaction, then, no depositors lose their funds. Table 1 illustrates the extensive use of this method of closure in Louisiana. In the other closure method listed, depositors are paid off directly by the FDIC; there is no merger of a healthy bank with the failed bank. The FDIC reports that virtually all depositors eventually receive the full amount of their deposits.

Table 1 also reports the amount of FDIC disbursements per year, giving an indication of the monetary magnitude of the problem, and the size of Louisiana's problems relative to the U.S. The final column of the table contains the total losses incurred by the FDIC per year, which confirms that the problem of bank failures is damaging the financial strength of the FDIC.

The federal government also regulates banks through the three agencies charged with protecting the safety of the banking system: the Federal Reserve System, the Office of the Comptroller of the Currency, and the FDIC. Traditionally, these agencies share supervisory responsibilities for banks: The Federal Reserve oversees banks that are state-chartered members of the Federal Reserve System; the Office of the Comptroller of the Currency governs banks that are nationally-chartered members of the Federal Reserve System; and the FDIC supervises all remaining (state-chartered, but not members of the Federal Reserve System) insured banks. The duties of these agencies involve formulation of detailed regulations and policies, on-site examinations of banks both for safety and for compliance with federal consumer-protection legislation, off-site reviews of reports submitted by banks, and closure of failed banks. Regulations defined by these agencies include the setting of the deposit interest rate ceiling (when one exists), designation of capital-to-asset ratios, imposition of limits to acceptable investments, and establishment of controls on loans.

With the legislative deregulation of the 1980's came a relaxation of regulations by the above-mentioned bank supervisory agencies, as well. The emphasis on less regulation led to a decline in direct supervision of banks by the agencies, as fewer on-site examinations were scheduled and fewer bank examiners employed. Figures 5 through 7 illustrate these declines over the years examined in the latter empirical work, 1974-89. Figures 5 and 6 show the ratio of safety examinations to total banks under the watch of the given agency; both the Federal Reserve System and the FDIC experienced decreases in the percentage of banks examined.[1] This downward trend reversed in the late 1980's as the government responded to the growing financial industry problems. The number of bank examiners employed is available only for the FDIC; Figure 7 shows that the downward trend is evident here as well, followed by an upsurge in employment when the financial system's problems grew large.

There were additional ways in which supervisory agencies eased their regulation of bank activities in the early 1980's. Regulations on bank lending limits were loosened, and so may have altered bank risk-taking. Lending limits place an upper limit on the amount a bank may loan to a single entity; this limit was raised from ten percent of bank capital to fifteen percent. Also in the early 1980's, banks were granted new powers of investment relating to real estate loans; the change allowed banks to make loans on undeveloped land, which was not previously allowed. Capital adequacy requirements (required capital-to-asset ratios) were revised several times, as well. During the late 1970's, the requirements were eased, but in the late 1980's the regulations were again tightened. Changes in regulations also may have affected the regulators and examiners. Those encountering the revised regulations would have discovered that the old "rule of thumb" decision rules used in bank examinations were now invalid. This would have produced a period of adjustment in which it was difficult for examiners and regulators to know whether they would be justified to take action against a bank and to know if they were effectively performing their jobs.

Changes in regulation developed at the state legislative level, as well as at the federal level. The data used in the empirical analysis of Chapters VII and VIII are from Louisiana, so noteworthy Louisiana regulations are mentioned here. The most important regulation imposed by the various states concerns branch-banking restrictions. Until 1985, banks in Louisiana could establish branch banks within their parish (county), but were not allowed to open branches across parish lines. A related state-imposed regulation concerns bank branching across state lines. No interstate branching was allowed during the time period covered by the data set. These branching regulations may limit banks in their ability to geographically diversify their portfolios, since their opportunities to provide loans may be constrained by the location of their offices. It is not illegal for banks to fund loans for investments outside of the parish or state; instead, it simply may be more difficult for banks to find this sort of loan opportunity when branching restrictions are in place.

Another important state regulatory action is the provision of a bank supervision department mandated by law to examine state-chartered banks; in Louisiana, this is the Commissioner of Banking and the Department of Financial Institutions. In practice, the supervision of state-chartered banks is shared with the Federal Reserve System and the FDIC, who hold primary responsibility for these banks' safety. Thus, either the state or one of the federal agencies examines a bank; there is no overlap.[2]

More recent changes in federal and state government intervention in the U.S. financial structure reflect ongoing debate over the cause of current U.S. financial industry problems. Originally, calls for regulatory reform emphasized the efficiency gains available; when the ensuing deregulation was accompanied by increased bank failures, discussion arose concerning the role of this deregulation in the bank failures. Most economists have agreed that fixed-rate deposit insurance is the primary culprit, but they are not unanimous on other regulatory issues.

A leading critic of the deposit insurance system is Kane, who presents a detailed criticism of that system and the moral hazard problem which accompanies it (Kane [1985]). He notes the difficulty of identifying problem banks that arises from accounting methods used by banks, as well as the dangers in purchase and assumption deals for closing failed banks. He recommends several changes to deposit insurance to lessen government (taxpayer) exposure to risk-taking, including changes in accounting procedures, a lower level of deposit insurance but one that would be uniformly enforced, and risk-based deposit insurance premiums.

Kareken [1981, 1983] also notes the moral hazard problem in the deposit insurance system, but he concentrates on a somewhat different aspect of the bank failure problem, deregulation of banks. He contends that the distortions in banks' risk choices caused by deposit insurance make government regulation essential; regulation is a "necessary complement" to, instead of a substitute for, deposit insurance. Given the structure of the deposit insurance program, deregulation of bank activities would be dangerous, he maintains. Allowing banks greater choice in investments or permitting expansion into related businesses would simply increase banks' opportunities to take on more risk.

O'Driscoll [1988] labels the preceding tenet the "sophisticated argument for regulating banks," but disputes its relevance for most regulations in place today. Rather than endorsing bank regulation, he supports further deregulation of banks. He believes that the current regulatory structure inhibits the ability of banks to diversify their portfolios properly; in particular, geographic restrictions and restrictions on investments prevent banks from adequately diversifying. He admits that banks that are allowed wider investment opportunities may choose to concentrate their portfolios in one specialty to increase their risk-taking, instead of diversifying to decrease their risk-taking. However, he asserts that under this scenario the financial system would, at worst, end up in the same position it is in now. He does not consider the possibility that giving banks expanded powers may also implicitly expand the federal government's responsibilities and taxpayers' potential liabilities.

Current problems in the financial system are due not to deregulation, but are the result of macroeconomic factors, aggravated by existing regulations that restrict banks, claims Eisenbeis [1986]. Like O'Driscoll, Eisenbeis believes that additional deregulation is required, since many of the regulations still in place promote bank risk-taking, instead of encouraging portfolio diversification. He also advises deposit insurance reform through a risk-based pricing policy and limits to insurance coverage. However, the primary cause of banking problems is the state of the macroeconomy; the existing regulations and deposit insurance structure simply intensify these problems by constraining bank responses to macroeconomic difficulties. My empirical work in Chapter VIII attempts to shed some light on this assertation.

There are many issues raised in these discussions of deregulation and in the facts of the regulatory changes. In the remainder of this book, I concentrate on the impact of deregulation on bank risk-taking. I later provide a simple model of a bank's choice of portfolio riskiness, and then examine the empirical implications of this model under the deregulation outlined in the above paragraphs.

Notes

1. The statistics for the Office of the Comptroller of the Currency are available for only a few years, so are not reported here.

2. I am unable to procure the actual number of examinations conducted by the state of Louisiana each year, so cannot estimate the percentage of state-chartered banks examined by the state over the years.

Figure 1

U.S. Bank Failures, 1934-89

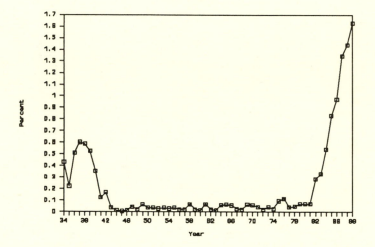

Figure 2

Louisiana Bank Failures, 1934-89

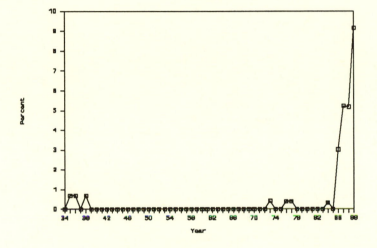

Figure 3

Deposits in Failed U.S. Banks

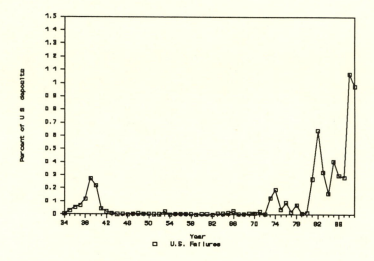

Figure 4

Deposits in Failed Louisiana Banks

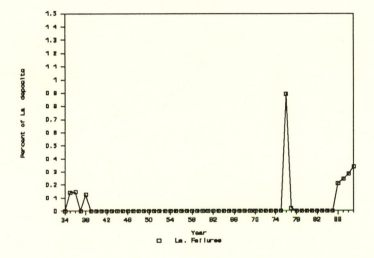

Figure 5

Bank Safety Examinations Conducted by Federal Reserve System

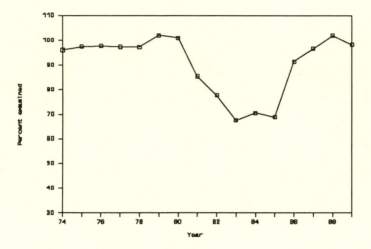

Figure 6

Bank Safety Examinations Conducted by FDIC

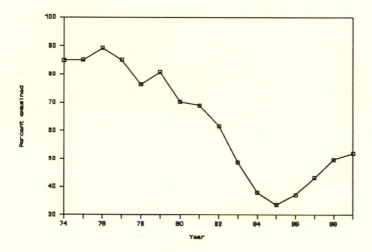

Figure 7

Bank Examiners Employed by FDIC

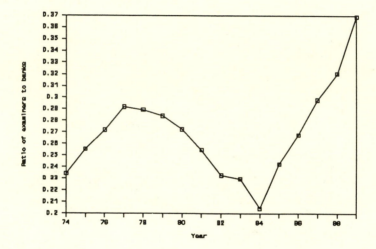

Table 1

Year	La. Bank Failures	FDIC Closure Methods		FDIC Disbursements			FDIC Losses
		Purchase and Assumption	Deposit Payoff	for La. (millions)	for U.S. (millions)	Percent in La.	for U.S. (millions)
1974	0	0	0	0	2403	0.0	0.039
1975	0	0	0	0	332	0.0	16
1976	1	1	0	117	599	19.5	0.247
1977	1	1	0	3	27	11.2	2
1978	0	0	0	0	546	0.0	9
1979	0	0	0	0	90	0.0	11
1980	0	0	0	0	152	0.0	31
1981	0	0	0	0	998	0.0	588
1982	0	0	0	0	2177	0.0	1284
1983	0	0	0	0	3544	0.0	1530

1984	1	0	1	37	7599	0.5	2010
1985	0	0	0	0	2714	0.0	908
1986	9	9	0	343	3959	8.7	1885
1987	15	15	0	275	4572	6.0	2120
1988	13	13	0	434	8175	5.3	4570
1989	21	20	1	750	8378	9.0	6090
TOTAL	60	58	2	1952	46265		21054

III. The Louisiana Economy, 1974-89

This chapter depicts the changes in the Louisiana economy between 1974 and 1989, the time period of the data set used in Chapters VII and VIII. The empirical tests there attempt to determine the causes of bank failures in this time period. One popular explanation is simply that a downturn in the local economy led to many business failures, including bank failures. It is important, then, to understand the fluctuations in the state economy, since this illustrates the historical setting in which the bank failures occurred.[1] In the following paragraphs, first, data on the gross state product create a general description of economic activity in Louisiana; next, two other economic indicators, the number of new houses authorized and the number of business failures, extend the analysis. Finally, data on employment and personal income levels are presented.

The annual gross state product (GSP) provides an overview of the state's economic health over most of the time period under investigation.[2] The GSP is equivalent to the gross domestic product on a national level. The total real GSP (in 1982 dollars) for Louisiana from 1974 through 1986 is charted in Figure 8, and its growth rate, in Figure 9. The real GSP for Louisiana grew each year from 1974 until 1981, the year in which it peaked. After 1981, real GSP declines each year except for 1984. In the years up to 1981, the growth rate of real GSP ranges from approximately one percent to eleven percent, with an average of seven percent; the negative growth rates after 1981 range from approximately two percent to nine percent, with an average of negative three percent. Thus, the real GSP data suggest that the Louisiana economy grew quite rapidly at times before 1981, but declined significantly after that.

The explanation for both the notable growth and the serious downturn lies in an examination of the major components of the Louisiana economy. Figure 10 summarizes the five largest sectors of this economy in 1977, a year of growth, and in 1986, a year of decline. The "oil and gas" category consists of both extraction of the minerals and the manufacture of derivative products, while "manufacturing" encompasses the total of all other manufacturing of durables and non-durables. Also, the data points labelled "transportation" includes that plus communication activities, and those labelled "finance" contain finance, insurance, and banking. Finally, "services" garners most of its value from tourist-related businesses.

In both 1977 and 1986, oil- and gas-related activities dominate the other segments of the economy, contributing almost thirty percent of the GSP in the earlier period, and only somewhat less, 23 percent, in the latter period. The next largest category, the total of other manufacturing, accounts for about fifteen percent of GSP in 1977, and twelve percent in 1986. The greatest change in contributions to GSP comes from oil and gas, which experiences a six percent decrease; the other contributions vary four percent or less between the two time periods. Nonetheless, Figure 10 portrays an economy dominated by the oil and gas industry in both the 1970's and the 1980's; shifts in the components of the economy are small.

Since the oil and gas industry dominates the Louisiana economy, a brief review of its fluctuations will provide some additional insights into the expansion and subsequent decline in Louisiana's economy. The story of oil prices in this time period is well-known. Annual average domestic crude oil prices, adjusted for inflation, are displayed in Figure 11. The crude oil price reaches its maximum in 1981, the year that Louisiana's real GSP does the same; the crude oil price plummets each year following 1981, while real GSP slides into negative growth rates. The price for crude oil eventually stabilizes around ten dollars per barrel in 1982 dollars, less than thirty percent of its uppermost value. This dramatic plunge in oil prices is a driving force behind the trends in the state economy, since the oil and gas industry directly contributes the largest share of the GSP value and indirectly affects other economic activity in the state.

Since the GSP data provides no information on the years after 1986, other measures of economic activity are needed to complete the picture of the Louisiana economy over the full time period. One economic indicator that is available for the entire time period is the annual number of housing units authorized by building permits; Figure 12 charts these numbers. Housing starts double between 1975 and 1976, and continue to climb through 1978; a slow decline follows this until a strong surge occurs in 1983, when housing starts reach their apex. Housing construction tumbles from approximately 29 thousand new homes in 1983 to eight thousand in 1986, and the downturn continues at a moderate pace through 1989. This evidence suggests that statewide economic activity continued its descent after 1986, although at a slower rate than before. Furthermore, new housing authorized in 1989 is about one-half the number of housing units authorized in 1974, so the economic downturn of the late 1980's is significant when compared not only to the economic boom of the early 1980's, but also to the early 1970's.

An additional indication of general economic activity that is available for the years 1974 through 1989 is the annual number of business failures statewide, which is a measure of the level of economic distress. Business failures as a proportion of total business establishments make up Figure 13. This graph confirms the conclusion drawn from Figure 12 (housing starts) that the state's economic slump persists through 1989. Relatively few businesses fail in each of the years before 1983; then the proportion of failures escalates almost unabated through 1989, the year in which the highest percentage of failures is recorded. The proportionate number of failures increases by a factor of ten between 1980 and 1989. The data on business failures, then, suggests that the state's economy suffered a persistent downward trend that had not yet bottomed out in the mid-1980's.

Additional evidence on the Louisiana economy's performance between 1974 and 1989 comes from personal income and employment data. Figure 14 displays the state's average annual unemployment numbers for this time period. Until 1981, unemployment in Louisiana remains fairly constant around seven percent; in 1981, it expands to eight and one-half percent, and eventually increases to the high annual average of thirteen percent in 1986. Even more startling is the parish-level data (used in the regressions later, but not presented here), which uncovers recurring unemployment rates of up to 25 percent in some parishes. Unlike the business failure data, however, the average unemployment figures depicted in Figure 14 drop each year after 1986, reaching eight percent in 1989. Thus, the unemployment data implies some improvement in the economy after 1986.

Finally, Figure 15 presents real personal income per capita for the years 1974 through 1988. Personal income gains steadily, occasionally in large steps, through 1981; it then levels off at approximately 10,200 dollars (in 1982 prices). Unlike the other economic variables presented here, real personal income remains fairly steady over the remainder of the decade. It declines somewhat in 1986 and 1987, but recovers in 1988; never does it return to the lower levels found in the mid-1970's. The data for real personal income only slightly reflect the economic crisis that the other economic variables indicate Louisiana experienced in the 1980's.

The economic gauges explored here generally establish that economic activity in Louisiana flourished until the early 1980's, mirroring the ascent of the price of oil. After this period of growth came a strong downturn, characterized by chronic high unemployment levels and a relatively high proportion of business failures. Only the real personal income data fail to display a major downturn, although the data do reveal a small decline. Both the business-failure rate and the housing-starts rate document that the economy had not yet recovered by 1989, while the unemployment rate suggests that recovery had begun. The importance of these macroeconomic variables in explaining bank portfolio risk and bank failures will be formally tested in the empirical work that follows.

Notes

1. The influence of the local economy will also be formally incorporated into the empirical tests.

2. Unfortunately, total GSP for Louisiana has not been published for any year after 1986.

Figure 8

Louisiana Real GSP

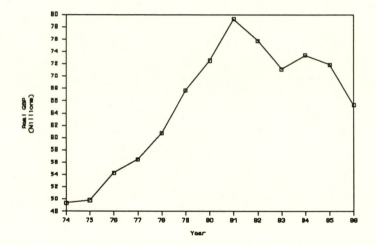

Figure 9

Real Growth Rate of Louisiana GSP

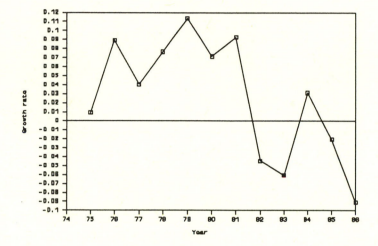

Figure 10

Louisiana Real GSP by Category

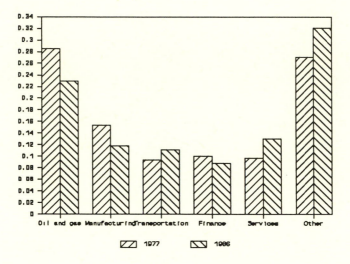

Figure 11

Real Domestic Crude Oil Prices
measured in 1982 dollars

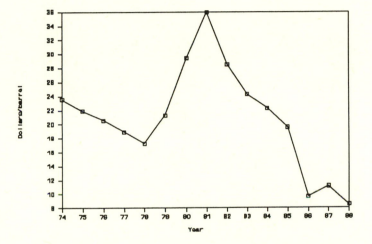

Figure 12

Housing Units Authorized by Building Permits

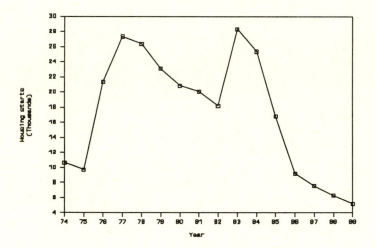

Figure 13

Louisiana Business Failures

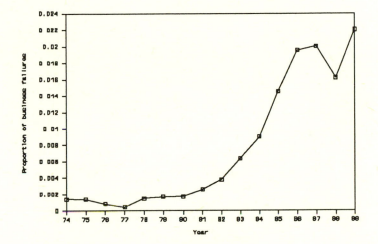

Figure 14

Louisiana Unemployment Rates

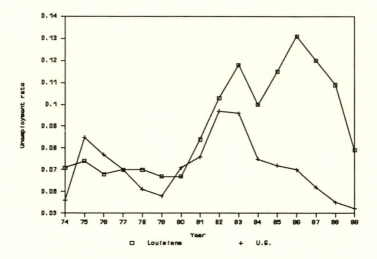

Figure 15

Louisiana Real Income per Capita

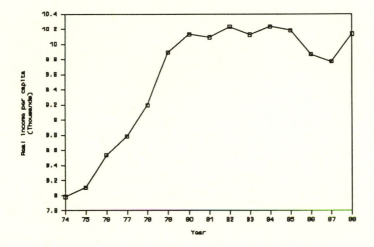

IV. Theories of Financial Stability

This chapter surveys theoretical and empirical work on financial stability and bank riskiness. Theoretical models of financial stability and the interconnected concern over the government's role in the financial system are examined first. Next, attempts to test empirically the effects of government intervention on bank risk choices are reviewed. A critical examination of previous measures of bank risk-taking leads to a proposal for an alternative measure of riskiness, which is described in detail in Chapter VI.

A. Theoretical Approaches

Why do banks fail? Theoretical explanations of bank failures conflict fundamentally. Two broad categories of explanations emerge: that banks fail because of government intervention, or that banks fail because of some endogenous instability. Theories in the former category argue that the financial system would be stable if there were no government interference; while theories in the latter category generally support government actions as stabilizing, not destabilizing. Since government intervention itself comprises one explanation of bank failures, the issue of the appropriate role of the government in the financial system is interdependent with the question of the cause of bank failures. These related issues, explanations of bank failures and the implications for the usefulness of government intervention, serve as the framework for the discussion that follows.

The case for government intervention as the cause of bank failures is presented by Kareken and Wallace [1978]. In this model, bank owners[1] face an unavoidable bankruptcy cost, which leads them to choose portfolios so that they do not fail in the laissez-faire equilibrium. Bank failures do occur when government provision of deposit insurance at a fixed cost to banks is introduced; this is an example of the moral hazard problem. Of course, in the laissez-faire model, there is no rationale for deposit insurance, since all deposits are completely safe without deposit insurance. If deposit insurance is offered nonetheless, regulations may prove useful in limiting additional bank risk-taking. However, in the Kareken and Wallace model, regulations are beneficial only in certain specific combinations. Capital-to-asset ratio requirements are not helpful when used alone, and ceilings on deposit interest rates are useful only when additional regulations accompany the ceiling.

Dothan and Williams [1980] analyze a similar model of banks that points to government intervention, specifically deposit insurance, as the cause of bank failures. They extend the analysis by analyzing variable-rate subsidized deposit insurance, and conclude that banks hold the same risky portfolios under this scheme that they hold with fixed-rate deposit insurance. This risk-taking can be offset simply by controlling a bank's portfolio composition and size; that is, it is necessary to constrain a bank to hold enough bonds (a risk-free security) to remain solvent in all states of the world. Furthermore, a ceiling on deposit interest rates is found to increase the probability of bankruptcy. As banks attempt to circumvent the ceiling, they increase services rendered to depositors; this reduces bank profits and increases the probability of bankruptcy. However, if a ceiling is combined with branching and entry restrictions, the ceiling becomes effective in reducing bankruptcies. This conclusion is quite similar to that of Kareken and Wallace [1978].

White [1984] also concludes that government intervention is inappropriate, although he considers a wider concept of government intervention in the financial system. In the White model, banks issue private money; no central bank exists, and the government does not supply money. Competition among banks constrains banks from taking excessive risks in investments, where portfolio risk arises from banks choosing how to divide investments between cash reserves and assets with a known return. The model does not explicitly incorporate uncertainty, so it cannot predict the choice of a bank when asset returns are uncertain. The banking system is stable, so regulations are not necessary in this environment.

Critics of the above models charge that some endogenous factor in the financial system is to blame for bank failures; this endogenous factor is not captured in the state-preference, complete capital market structure used by Kareken and Wallace [1978] and

Dothan and Williams [1980]. In simple state-preference models with complete markets, banks and money are unnecessary. It is this problem that has motivated the search for a different model of the financial system. The precise endogenous factor that produces the financial instability differs among these later models, and several possibilities are explored in the papers reviewed below.

Friedman [1960] argues that U.S. financial institutions face a "problem of 'inherent instability.'" The financial system is not stable because banks hold less than one hundred percent reserves on their deposits; this practice leaves banks vulnerable to bank runs. Government intervention in the form of federally-provided deposit insurance is useful, Friedman argues, because it removes the incentive for depositors to begin a run. Regulation of deposit interest rates, however, serves no purpose in controlling the instability; it is simply a government interference in market prices. Friedman advocates a new regulation requiring banks to hold one hundred percent reserves on their deposits; with this new requirement, deposit insurance would be unnecessary. However, as Diamond and Dybvig [1986] have subsequently pointed out, this new requirement would prevent banks from performing their principal service, namely, creating liquidity.

Minsky [1977] believes that instability occurs for a different reason. In Minsky's framework, a robust financial system automatically moves to "systemic fragility." He defines a fragile financial system as one in which "continued normal functioning can be disrupted by some not unusual event," and theorizes that the form of financing in the present U.S. financial structure breeds fragility. As optimism increases, financing progresses from hedge financing, when a firm has sufficient income in each period to service debt payments in that period; to speculative financing, wherein a firm has positive net worth but does not have income to cover debt payments in each period; and finally, to Ponzi financing, when a firm borrows increasing amounts to cover its debt payments. Minsky concludes that a lender of last resort is necessary to lessen the impact of financial fragility when it arises.

Kindleberger [1989] utilizes an adapted version of the Minsky theory of endogenous instability to explain cycles of crises in history. He traces the history of financial crises through several hundred years and observes that the crises share many features. Crises arise naturally from bank overexpansion of credit, or "overtrading," at a point of too-high optimism. Historical episodes of financial distress demonstrate that rapid expansion of bank credit is a typical precursor of financial crises;

Kindleberger implicitly argues that rapid expansion corresponds to greater risk-taking by banks. He finds strong support for government intervention from a lender of last resort. Deposit insurance is a rule-based form of lender of last resort; this leads to problems of moral hazard that can be avoided with a discretionary lender of last resort. Other regulations are less effective and the effectiveness depends on the vigilance of the regulators; yet regulators cannot control the optimism that drives the overexpansion, Kindleberger maintains.

Like Minsky, Heymann and Leijonhufvud [1989] consider financing to be the key to fragile financial systems. Financial fragility arises simply because economic agents are linked through the extension of credit to one another; fragility is present because of the "dense web of such endless chains of conditional promises." A crisis develops endogenously when miscalculations of investment opportunities or some other trigger leads to a break in the chain of credit, which prompts the contraction of the web of credit. As credits (loans) are called in, not only those agents who are insolvent, but also those who are illiquid are caught, which adds to the uncertainty in the economy. (The distinction between insolvency and illiquidity here corresponds to Minsky's Ponzi and speculative financing.) This, in turn, is a "deviation-amplifying process" that prolongs the disequilibrium in the economy. A role for the government in preventing this scenario is not discussed, but it is suggested that a central bank, as lender of last resort, may sort the illiquid from the insolvent more accurately than individual agents could sort them.

The theories advanced by Minsky, Kindleberger, and Heymann and Leijonhufvud share some common themes. All doubt that the assumption of complete markets is an appropriate starting point for a model of financial crisis. The theories also challenge the assumption of rational expectations; Kindleberger and Heymann and Leijonhufvud do so explicitly, while Minsky does this implicitly through his reliance on "optimism" to move the market from hedge financing to other less-stable forms of financing. In contrast, the following model addresses panics that may arise when agents respond rationally to new information.

In the influential paper by Diamond and Dybvig [1983], endogenous instability arises because speculative bank runs occur. In the three-period model, banks invest in riskless, but illiquid assets; that is, one-period investment returns are low, while two-period returns are high.[2] Agents are uncertain in the initial period about the desired timing of later consumption; when they discover the desired time in the second period, this information remains private. If confidence in banks falters, a "bad" equilibrium with bank runs will occur. Even those agents who prefer to consume later will try to withdraw now, since depositors are paid out sequentially and the illiquidity of a bank's portfolio implies that not all depositors can be paid. Diamond and Dybvig find that a deposit insurance scheme which severs the dependence of deposit payouts on the volume of withdrawals is welfare-improving.[3] This model is interesting because it formally models a "panic" while retaining the assumption of rational expectations of agents.

Finally, Smith [1984] develops a model that concentrates on competition for deposits instead of endogenous riskiness. "Inherent instability" of the financial system in this model corresponds to the non-existence of a Nash equilibrium in the model. Banks compete for deposits from depositors whose probabilities of withdrawal of the deposits differ; additionally, these probabilities are known only to the depositors. An adverse selection problem arises, and there is no Nash equilibrium in the model unless a deposit interest rate ceiling is imposed. Government intervention, then, is crucial, since establishing a deposit interest rate ceiling controls the system's instability. Other government action, like the provision of deposit insurance, is unnecessary. This model differs from others in that portfolio risk choices are not a reason for instability; the model is limited by its lack of analysis of this component of financial instability.

My model in Chapter V will investigate the link between bank risk-taking and regulation, augmenting the hypothesis mentioned by Kareken and Wallace [1978] and advanced more fully by Kareken [1983]: Deposit insurance provided by the government at a flat-rate fee encourages additional risk-taking by banks; this distortion can be offset through regulation of banks. Specifically, I demonstrate that a ceiling on interest rates paid on deposits may limit riskiness. My model differs from Smith [1984] in that it focuses on bank riskiness, and includes deposit insurance in the model. Smith's model derives its results without reference to bank riskiness, and without the presence of deposit insurance. Also, unlike Dothan and Williams [1980], the simple model of Chapter V concludes that an interest rate ceiling is an effective limit on risk-taking.

B. Empirical Approaches

Direct empirical tests of a possible link between financial stability and regulation are not numerous. As government regulations changed over the past two decades, several studies addressed the impact of these changes on banks in terms of wealth transfers among banks; the few investigations which include analysis of the impact of these changes on bank riskiness will be discussed below. Other empirical work that is related to financial stability concerns prediction of bank failures; since these works attempt to isolate causes of bank failures, the riskiness of bank portfolios is usually examined. Recent examples of this work will also be summarized below.

What do empirical tests of the effects of government regulation on bank riskiness show? Allen and Wilhelm [1988] find no significant changes in risk for large, Federal Reserve member banks before and after deregulation, based on an analysis of daily returns to the stocks of these banks.[4] This study uses the "beta" from the capital asset pricing model to measure risk before and after the enactment date for the 1980 Depository Institution Deregulation and Monetary Control Act (DIDMCA). However, their sample ends only thirty weeks after deregulation, so the empirical results may be misleading. The effects of deregulation would not be incorporated fully by banks in this limited thirty-week time period; additionally, if investors are uncertain about the effects of deregulation, the market would reflect this uncertainty in the short run.

Smirlock [1984] analyzes the effects of government regulation of interest rates specifically. Using data on large, publicly-traded banks, he tests the impact of interest-rate regulatory changes on bank systematic risk, again the "beta" from the capital asset pricing model; and on bank total risk, the variance of the banks' stock returns. These two measures are calculated for a sixty-day time period before and a sixty-day period after the announcement of the regulatory change. The tests suggest that interest rate deregulation has no effect on either measure of bank riskiness. Unfortunately, the time period examined does not encompass the important changes in regulations that occurred in 1980, nor does it cover an extended time period around each event.

Rolnick [1987], on the other hand, supplies evidence that is supportive of government regulation of deposit interest rates to control bank risk-taking. Using data from the 1920's, he discovers a positive relationship between bank riskiness and deposit interest rates, quantified in a simple regression relating measures of the former to the latter. The risk measures employed in this study include the capital-to-asset ratio and the loan-to-deposit ratio. Of course, deposit insurance was not present in the 1920's, so the results of his work are not fully applicable to the present U.S. financial system.

The consequences of government regulation for bank risk-taking have not been explicitly incorporated into empirical models of bank failures. Explanations of recent U.S. bank failures usually include reference to local economic activity and individual bank management. Gunther [1989] investigates troubled-asset-to-total-asset ratios for Texas banks by dividing banks into an aggressively managed group and a conservatively managed group. He finds that the troubled-asset ratios are explained by both declining economic conditions and aggressive management of banks. A useful feature of this study is that it controls for differences among bank size, location, and age; yet, it does not address the possible impact of deregulation or interest rate expenses on bank problems. Short and Gunther [1988] evaluate the condition of Texas thrifts. The principal causes of thrift problems are determined to be low asset quality, as measured by the level of problem loans, and higher interest rate expenses; but the direct impact of these variables on the probability of failure is not explored.

Avery and Hanweck [1984] conclude that various financial ratios are good predictors of bank failures, including the capital-to-asset ratio, the ratio of loans to assets, and the proportion of commercial loans in the loan portfolio. This study does not investigate the implications of deregulation; in fact, the data set used merges observations from the regulated time period and the deregulated time period without regard for institutional changes over the two periods. The estimated model, therefore, does not allow for changes in the relationship between bank failures and the included explanatory variables.

An indirect approach to determining the impact of deregulation on bank failures is the bank failure prediction model of Pantalone and Platt [1987]. They construct a model with profitability, leverage, risk, and the state economy as explanatory variables, and compare it to earlier bank failure prediction models. They conclude that "the principal cause of bank failure remains the same as in earlier decades, namely poor bank management."[5]   The state economy had little effect on failures, but risk-taking was positively related to the probability of failure. This work is innovative in its use of a maximum likelihood logit model; it does not, however, allow for possible simultaneity among variables, nor does it account for the effects of deregulation on risk-taking.

The measurement of bank portfolio riskiness, a critical element of the empirical tests, poses a problem for the above studies. Pantalone and Platt [1987] and Rolnick [1987] use measures such as the ratio of total loans to total assets and the ratio of commercial and industrial loans to total loans as risk measures. Avery and Hanweck [1984] adopt the ratio of net loan charge-offs (loan losses) to total loans as an additional risk measure. Gunther [1989] creates a risk index using principal-components analysis of five asset categories: commercial and industrial loans, construction loans, government securities, large certificates of deposit, and net federal funds purchased. However, the loan ratios used in these papers are insufficient measures of diversification and risk. They do not account for covariance among the returns to the categories. If various loan categories react in the same way to shocks in the economy, then a bank's loan portfolio may be quite risky even though the portfolio is not concentrated in any one category. Boyd and Graham [1986] employ the standard deviation of the return on assets to improve the measurement of riskiness; however, it is averaged across years, so that intertemporal changes in risk are impossible to identify. Smirlock's [1984] choice of "beta" does capture the covariance of returns among various assets; while the variance of daily bank stock returns quantifies risk more comprehensively. In Chapter VI.B.1, I propose an improved measure of bank riskiness based on beta; additionally, I investigate some measures of total risk.

My empirical work offers new insights in several respects. It creates an improved measure of bank riskiness that accounts for the covariances of returns in bank portfolios. Also, the empirical tests build upon the works of Pantalone and Platt [1987] and Gunther [1989] by allowing deregulation and interest rate expenses to affect bank loan portfolio riskiness, along with other variables. It differs from Rolnick [1987] by examining the risk and interest-rate relationship under different institutional conditions, namely, the presence of deposit insurance. Finally, my empirical tests use a comprehensive unbalanced panel of individual banks to provide a data set that spans the years 1974-89, covering both regulation and deregulation in the sample period.

Notes

1. Bank managers are not included in this model, so a principal-agent problem does not arise.

2. There is some similarity between this definition and Minsky's definition of speculative financing. However, in the Diamond-Dybvig model, assets are riskless, while in the Minsky theory assets are risky.

3. Wallace [1988] contends that the Diamond-Dybvig deposit insurance plan is not feasible because it violates the model's assumption that agents withdraw deposits in a random sequential order. However, it seems that Diamond and Dybvig do recognize this, since it is the purpose of deposit insurance to violate the sequential-order constraint; that is what makes deposit insurance welfare-improving over the equilibrium solution without deposit insurance.

4. In a related study, Cornett and Tehranian [1990] detect positive abnormal returns for large banks and negative abnormal returns for small banks from the 1982 deregulation act, by examining daily stock returns on about 230 financial institutions. They do not examine possible changes in riskiness.

5. A study of management technique by the U.S. Comptroller of the Currency (1988) concurs that the "caliber of management" was the most important characteristic distinguishing failed from healthy banks. It does not discuss the possible connection between a bank's choice of risk and deregulation.

V. A Model of Bank Risk-taking

This section develops a simple model of the Kareken [1983] argument that regulation helps to control excessive risk-taking in banks. The model illustrates the moral hazard problem inherent in fixed-rate deposit insurance, and the risk-limiting effect of government regulation, in this case, deposit interest rate ceilings. It demonstrates the way in which deregulation may have significantly affected the probability of bank failures. It differs from the model of Smith [1984] by emphasizing bank riskiness and the impact of interest rate regulation on the bank's risk decision.

Provision of fixed-rate deposit insurance means that the government pays for any deficit between the value of a bank's investments and its deposit liabilities. This introduces the well-recognized moral hazard problem in a bank's decisions. Roughly speaking, a bank takes increased risks because the bank gains from the possible increased positive returns, and the government, not the bank, loses from the possible increased loss. As I will show, in the presence of this deposit insurance, an increase in the interest paid by a bank on deposits, ceteris paribus, will increase a bank's choice of investment risk. Higher deposit interest rates paid by a bank, relative to the return on its investments, cause a bank to consider less of the downside risk of its investments, and it will thus choose riskier investments. This implies that a binding ceiling on deposit interest rates can be an effective limit on bank risk-taking, because it compels the bank to include a larger portion of the asset return distribution in its decision-making (including more of the downside risk). An effective deposit interest rate ceiling, then, reduces the magnitude of the moral hazard problem.

The model considers the decisions of a risk-neutral bank confronting a one-period profit maximization problem. The bank earns an uncertain return on its investments, R. It chooses a level of riskiness for its portfolio, denoted by Θ. The bank also accepts deposits on which it pays the return $(1 + r)$.[1] To simplify the model, the bank's capital is set equal to zero, and asset and deposit quantities are normalized to one. Deposits at banks are credibly guaranteed from loss by the risk-neutral government. There is no upper limit on the amount of deposit insurance.[2]

The uncertain return on a bank's portfolio is characterized by a probability density function, $g(R,\Theta)$, conditional on the choice of riskiness, Θ. Let the mean of R given Θ be represented by $M(\Theta)$. In what follows, the derivative of g with respect to Θ will be denoted by g_2. In order to define riskiness, $g(R,\Theta)$ is restricted as follows:

Condition 1: For each Θ, there exists a value α, $\alpha > 0$, such that
  i) $g_2(R,\Theta) > 0$ if $R < M(\Theta) - \alpha$
  ii) $g_2(R,\Theta) < 0$ if $M(\Theta) - \alpha < R < M(\Theta) + \alpha$
  iii) $g_2(R,\Theta) > 0$ if $R > M(\Theta) + \alpha$

This condition specifies that increasing Θ increases risk in the sense that the variance of the probability density function will increase. An increase in risk moves some of the weight from the center of the density function to the tails of the density function.

What is the socially optimal choice of riskiness? The objective is to maximize expected returns:

$$(1) \qquad \max_{\Theta} E(R) = \int_{-\infty}^{\infty} R \cdot g(R,\Theta)dR \ .$$

The socially optimal choice of riskiness, Θ^*, is defined by the first order condition[3]

$$(2) \qquad \int_{-\infty}^{\infty} R \cdot g_2(R,\Theta)dR = 0.$$

Now assume that the government provides deposit insurance, so that the government pays any deficit between the bank's realized return on its portfolio, R, and the bank's payout on deposits, $(1 + r)$. The bank considers this profit maximization problem:

(3)
$$\pi = -F + \int_{(1+r)}^{\infty} [R - (1 + r)] \cdot g(R,\Theta)dR ,$$

where F is the bank's fixed costs. The bank's choice of Θ when deposit insurance is present, Θ', is defined by the first order condition

(4)
$$\int_{(1+r)}^{\infty} [R - (1 + r)] \cdot g_2(R,\Theta)dR = 0 .$$

To clarify the impact of deposit insurance in this model, consider the choice function for the bank if fixed-rate deposit insurance were not provided. Under this scenario, the rate paid on deposits by the bank, $(1 + r)$, is a function of its risk choice, Θ. Let r_1 denote the first derivative of $r(\Theta)$; then $r_1 > 0$, since depositors demand a higher return for higher-risk investments. A bank then faces the following profit maximization function[4]:

(3')
$$\pi = -F + \int_{(1+r)}^{\infty} \{R - [1 + r(\Theta)]\} \cdot g(R,\Theta)dR ,$$

The first order condition for the choice of Θ, designated by Θ'', now includes an additional term:

(4')
$$\int_{(1+r)}^{\infty} - r_1(\Theta) \cdot g(R,\Theta)dR$$
$$+ \int_{(1+r)}^{\infty} \{R - [(1 + r(\Theta))]\} \cdot g_2(R,\Theta)dR = 0.$$

The essential difference, then, between the objective function with deposit insurance and this function with no deposit insurance, is the dependence of $(1 + r)$ on Θ in the latter case.

It will now be established that when deposit insurance is present, a bank chooses a higher level of risk than is socially optimal.

Proposition 1: Given $(1 + r) < M(\Theta^*) - \alpha$, when deposit insurance is present, a bank chooses a portfolio with more risk than the social optimum; that is, $\Theta' > \Theta^*$.

Proof: We wish to compare equations (2) and (4), which define the choice of riskiness, Θ, in each case. To do so, we rewrite equation (2) by noting that, since g is a probability density function,

$$(5) \qquad \int_{-\infty}^{\infty} g_2(R,\Theta)dR = 0.$$

Multiplying (5) by $(1 + r)$ and subtracting it from (2) gives this alternate expression for the social-optimum first order conditions:

$$(6a) \qquad \int_{-\infty}^{\infty} [R - (1 + r)]g_2(R,\Theta)dR = 0 \, ,$$

or

$$(6b) \qquad \int_{-\infty}^{(1+r)} [R - (1 + r)]g_2(R,\Theta)dR$$

$$+ \qquad \int_{(1+r)}^{\infty} [R - (1 + r)]g_2(R,\Theta)dR = 0.$$

Given $(1 + r) < M(\Theta^*) - \alpha$, the first integral of equation (6b) is negative in sign; this implies that the second integral is positive in sign. But the second integral is the same as equation (4). This integral is greater than zero in the social optimum, but is equal to zero for bank profit maximization with deposit insurance; therefore, since the bank's objective function is concave, Θ' as defined in (4) is greater than Θ^* as defined in (2).[5] ◄

Proposition 1 depicts the moral hazard problem that is often cited in criticisms of deposit insurance. That is, with deposit insurance, a bank chooses a portfolio that is riskier than the social optimum because the bank will profit from the possible additional gains, but will not pay if there are additional losses. The restriction that

$(1 + r) < M(\Theta^*) - \alpha$ ensures that a bank choosing additional riskiness will face an increased probability of extreme returns. The extreme returns are desirable to the bank, because it gains higher probability of greater positive returns, but does not lose from the higher probability of greater negative returns. Instead, the government absorbs this additional downside risk.

The government may attempt to counteract the moral hazard problem through regulation of banks. One possibility is direct regulation of bank investments by limiting investment opportunities to certain "safe" categories, or by limiting the amount of investments in any one category. The appropriate definition of safe investments presents a difficulty in the practical application of this approach; furthermore, confining a bank to a certain set of investment opportunities may shrink its opportunities for diversification. Another regulatory possibility is direct supervision of banks through inspections and examinations of the bank's investment portfolio by government regulators. Examinations of banks should be frequent and detailed if they are to be effective. (Chapter II offers evidence that examinations decreased with deregulation.) Another alternative is regulation of interest rates paid on deposits. The usefulness of this regulation is investigated next.

Does a ceiling imposed on the return to deposits affect the bank's choice of riskiness? In this model, we can show that an increase in $(1 + r)$ relative to the return on bank investments leads to an increase in Θ. If the removal of a ceiling causes the interest rate on deposits to rise, a bank's choice of riskiness will also rise. In this way, deregulation leads to increased risk-taking by banks.

Proposition 2: Given $(1 + r) < M(\Theta') - \alpha$, an increase in $(1 + r)$ will lead to an increase in Θ.

Proof: We shall determine that the derivative of (4) with respect to $(1 + r)$ is positive. This derivative is

$$(7a) \qquad \int_{(1+r)}^{\infty} -g_2(R,\Theta)dR$$

which may be divided into

(7b) $\int_{(1+r)}^{M(\Theta')-\alpha} -g_2(R,\Theta)dR + \int_{M(\Theta')-\alpha}^{\infty} -g_2(R,\Theta)dR$.

Using equality (5) again, we see that

(8) $\int_{-\infty}^{M(\Theta')-\alpha} -g_2(R,\Theta)dR + \int_{M(\Theta')-\alpha}^{\infty} -g_2(R,\Theta)dR = 0$.

Given $(1 + r) < M(\Theta') - \alpha$, the first integral in equations (7b) and (8) is negative. For equation (8), this implies that the second integral is positive. The second integral in equation (7b) equals the second integral in (8), so it is also positive. The first integral in (7b) is a smaller negative value than that in (8). Therefore, since (8) equals zero, (7b) must be greater than zero. ◄

Proposition 2 illustrates the impact of one type of government regulation on bank riskiness. With deposit insurance, a bank is concerned with only the portion of the asset return distribution that lies above $(1 + r)$, since the government assumes the bank's obligations if asset returns fall below $(1 + r)$. Proposition 2 shows that as a bank pays higher interest rates on deposits, holding constant the return rate on bank assets, the bank considers smaller regions of the asset return distribution function; since the bank considers less of the downside risk than before, it chooses riskier investments. Or, considering this conclusion in reverse, it means that imposing a binding ceiling on deposit interest rates causes a bank to choose less-risky investments by inducing the bank to incorporate a larger part of the downside risk in its decision-making.

The strength of this relationship between risk and deposit interest rates depends on the institutional, or regulatory, structure of the time. Regulated banks face similar deposit interest rate costs when the interest rate ceiling is binding, so banks facing a binding interest rate ceiling would be expected to show little variation in interest rates paid; differences in interest rates paid would reflect differences in deposit maturities. However, banks that are not constrained by an interest rate ceiling would choose riskier investments as the deposit rate paid increases relative to the return on bank investments. The risk-deposit rate relationship, then, should be positive in the deregulated time period.

In summary, this model establishes that a bank with fixed-rate deposit insurance chooses a higher-risk portfolio than is socially optimal. A ceiling on deposit interest rates mitigates risk-taking. The model formalizes the argument that government regulation of banks may be necessary, given the present deposit insurance system. The theoretical model developed in this chapter will guide the empirical model specification in Chapters VII and VIII.

Notes

1. This model does not explain the determination of a competitive market deposit interest rate; extension of the model in this way should not alter the primary results.

2. The FDIC's actions in closing failed banks generally have led to de facto unlimited deposit insurance coverage; see Chapter II for evidence on this issue.

3. It will be assumed that the solution lies in the range where the second order condition for a maximum holds, $g_{22}(R,\Theta) < 0$, so that the objective function is concave in Θ.

4. Since the model assumes that a bank holds no capital, this objective function is equivalent to one considered by a firm that is completely debt-financed.

5. Similar relations can be established with Θ'' defined in equation (4'). Appendix A demonstrates that $\Theta^* < \Theta'' < \Theta'$.

VI. Construction of the Data Set

What is the empirical evidence on financial stability and deregulation? The remainder of the book confronts this question. This chapter specifies the contents of the data set used in the empirical tests of Chapters VII and VIII; it also considers the issues of measuring the variables of primary concern, bank risk and deposit interest rates. In the following sections, first, the data will be described. Next, the deficiencies in traditional risk measures are illustrated; this critique motivates the definition of three alternative measures of bank risk-taking, all of which are calculable for the banks in the sample data set. The pseudo-beta measure defined in this section is new to the empirical work on bank risk-taking behavior. An examination of the other critical variable, the deposit interest rate, constitutes the final section.

A. The Data on Individual Banks

The empirical work which follows uses annual data on individual banks in Louisiana for the period 1974-1989. The data come from bank Statement of Condition and Income reports, or "call reports," which are filed by all banks with the federal government.[1] These reports include a balance sheet, an income statement, and other specialized material on bank activities.

The sample is limited to banks in just one state to eliminate effects resulting from differences in regulations across states. For example, bank portfolios will be affected by regulations on branch banking that vary among states. Louisiana banks were chosen since the Louisiana economy experienced both rapid growth and severe recession in the sample period; the usual explanation for the record bank failures there is that the economic downturn hurt bank profitability. I will attempt to determine whether deregulation also played a part through its effect on bank portfolio riskiness.

Information on each bank's loan portfolio consists of the total quantity of loans and the percentage of the portfolio invested in various categories established by the Federal Reserve. These categories are listed in the Data Appendix. Information on each bank's liabilities was also collected. It consists of the total quantity of deposits for each bank, and the total interest expense on deposits for each bank. The data set also contains a measure of bank profitability, the ratio of net income to total assets; and a leverage measure, the capital-to-total-asset ratio.

Some information is also available on non-performing loans, defined as loans that are 90 or more days past due plus non-accruing loans. The percentage of non-performing loans in four broad categories, agriculture, real estate, commercial, and individual loans, is available for 1986-89. For all years, a scaled net charge-off figure and a scaled loan loss reserve figure are available. The net charge-off amount is that portion of loans actually declared as a loss, net of any recoveries on non-performing loans. This may serve as an ex post measure of loan quality, or portfolio riskiness. The loan loss reserve is an amount put aside by the bank to absorb future bad loans, so is an ex ante measure in that it measures the bank's expectation of the amount of future non-performing loans.

B. Choosing an Appropriate Risk Measure

1.   The Pseudo-Beta Measure

Measuring bank riskiness accurately is an important component of the empirical tests to follow. Empirical work on bank riskiness traditionally uses measures like the loan-to-total-asset ratio, or the proportion of loans in a certain category (for example, real estate construction loans) that is deemed an especially risky category. Finance theory suggests that a better measure of riskiness is the capital asset pricing model "beta," which accounts for covariances among assets.[2] Beta is defined as the covariance of an asset's returns with the market's returns, scaled by the variance of market returns. The beta for a portfolio is the weighted sum of the betas for each asset in the portfolio. This concept of risk measurement is better than measures that use just one loan category to quantify risk because it captures the interdependence of returns among loans in all the categories of the loan portfolio. For example, a portfolio with investments in many categories with high, but uncorrelated, risks will be less risky than a portfolio with highly-correlated investments.

A beta is usually constructed for an asset like a stock by computing the covariance of its daily returns with that of the daily returns on a stock market index. The banks in the sample in this book generally do not trade on active markets, so this option is not available. Similarly, daily returns on each bank's loan portfolio are not reported; the only information available is an annual net-income-to-total-assets ratio. Since the focus here is on changes in beta from year to year, this annual information is not sufficient for calculation of the necessary covariances. Instead, a pseudo-beta is constructed for each bank's loan portfolio by using proxies for returns to the bank's various loan categories. The proxies used for these loan categories are betas calculated from equity market returns for industries that are similar to the loan categories. The Data Appendix describes the proxy employed for each loan category. The pseudo-beta for the loan portfolio of bank i in year t is

$$\text{ß}_{it} = \Sigma\, \text{ß}_{jt}\cdot w_{ijt}\,,$$

where ß_{jt} is the beta proxy for loan category j in year t, and w_{ijt} is the weight of loan category j in the total portfolio of bank i in year t. The pseudo-beta is one of the measures used below to analyze bank risk-taking behavior.

Pseudo-beta calculates measures of bank portfolio risk that generally accord with market betas. To learn more about the nature of the pseudo-beta, Figures 16 and 17 compare the annual sample mean pseudo-beta with two annual market betas, the betas for state-chartered banks and for bank holding companies listed on the New York Stock Exchange. The range of the annual mean pseudo-betas resembles that of the annual market betas, although the market betas oscillate more. The smaller range of pseudo-beta compared to market betas suggests that pseudo-beta is a conservative estimate of bank portfolio risk.

The main deviations between the pseudo-beta and the market betas occur in 1986 and 1987; interestingly, beta for the state-chartered banks escalates, while beta for the bank holding companies falls. These strong movements in the market beta most likely reflect the market's incorporation of new information concerning the extent of the banking crisis in the U.S. (Figure 1 shows that in 1986 bank failures in the U.S. soared to one percent of total banks for the first time.) The pseudo-beta, on the other hand, falls slightly in this time period, while rising in the early 1980's, just after deregulation. It is not surprising that the sample pseudo-betas do not mimic exactly the market beta movements, since pseudo-betas detect riskiness for individual Louisiana banks; that is, the average large bank traded on the NYSE is not expected to be exactly like the average bank in the sample drawn from Louisiana.

One bank in the sample data set, Hibernia Bank, does trade on an organized market, so the market beta and the pseudo-beta for Hibernia can be compared directly. Figures 18 and 19 graph the two risk measures in absolute terms and in first differences, respectively. As Figure 18 reveals, the absolute value of pseudo-beta is larger than the market beta each year until 1985, after which it remains smaller than the market beta. While this graph shows differences in the absolute magnitude between the two measures, it suggests that the movement of the two measures is similar; therefore, Figure 19 graphs the measures in terms of annual changes. The measures do move in comparable ways in this figure, although pseudo-beta changes seem to lag behind market beta changes by about a year; only the years 1983 and 1985-86 exhibit little correspondence between the movements in the two measures. Overall, the course followed by pseudo-beta for Hibernia Bank mimics the movements in the market beta.

2.   The Pseudo-Variance Measure

Although the pseudo-beta based on the CAPM quantifies systematic risk and establishes the usefulness of considering covariation among assets in evaluating the riskiness of a portfolio, it is not a measure of total risk, which includes both systematic and unsystematic risk. In the empirical tests to follow, it will be helpful to consider this comprehensive concept of risk, as well as the systematic risk. Since the empirical work is motivated by a search for explanations of recent bank failures, it is likely that a measure of total risk will be pertinent. This is because a bank's failure should be more closely related to the total risk it faces than to systematic risk alone. The theoretical model of Chapter V is in terms of total risk; the moral hazard problem illustrated therein provides banks with an incentive to increase total risk, not just systematic risk. The measures of total risk, then, offer additional insight into the problem. Two proxies for total risk are discussed next.

One popular proxy for the total risk of an asset is the variance of its returns in an equity market. The variance incorporates both the portion of risk that moves with the market, systematic risk, and the unsystematic risk. The variance of a stock, like the beta, is usually constructed from daily returns to that stock. Again, since the banks in my sample do not trade daily on the market, it is necessary to construct a proxy, or pseudo-variance measure, for each bank; it is assembled in much the same way as the pseudo-beta. However, the variance of a portfolio of many assets is the weighted sum of both the variances of the assets in the portfolio, plus the covariances between the assets in the portfolio, so proxies for both are formulated. For each loan category each year, the variance and covariance proxies for that category are calculated using the returns of the same equity market proxy used in making the pseudo-beta. The pseudo-variance, then, for the portfolio of bank i in year t is

$$\upsilon_{it} = \mathbf{W' \cdot \Sigma \cdot W} ,$$

where $\mathbf{W}$ is a 1 x n matrix of the proportions of bank i's portfolio held in n loan categories in year t, and Σ is the n x n variance-covariance matrix for the returns to the proxies for the n loan categories for year t. Estimates of this measure of variance will be used in the empirical work to follow.

Figures 20 and 21 compare the annual average estimated pseudo-variance to the annual variance of market returns on state-chartered banks and on bank holding companies, respectively. Figure 20 shows that pseudo-variance displays some connection to the returns on state-chartered banks in the early years, although the measures occasionally diverge; in later years, however, especially beginning in 1986, the market variance rockets above its earlier levels. Figure 21 portrays a similar pattern, with the bank holding company variance first leaping sharply in 1984. This drastic shift in market variances in the mid-1980's is comparable to that seen in the graphs of the market betas, Figures 16 and 17; as mentioned in the discussion of those figures, these market swings may be due to market incorporation of new information about the banking crisis.

Figure 22 contrasts the annual pseudo-variance for Hibernia National Bank with the annual variance of its market returns. Like the other market measures, Hibernia's market variance climbs sharply in the mid-1980's, mostly in 1986 and 1987. Until 1982, pseudo-variance and the market-returns variance follow each other fairly closely; after that, the measures deviate. Generally, Figures 20 through 22 show that pseudo-variance provides a reasonable estimate of the variance of bank returns; often, though, it does not closely imitate movements in market returns. This shortcoming may be reflected in the regression results that follow.

3.   The Probability-of-Failure Measure

A second, perhaps more direct, means of assessing total risk comes from the fact that some banks did fail over the time period under examination. This information may be effectively incorporated into another measure of total risk. This alternative definition of total risk, then, will be the final outcome of each bank in the sample, where the outcome is either bank failure or bank survival. If a bank fails at some point in the sample, its status is one for the entire sample period; otherwise, its status is zero. Failure is defined as FDIC closure of the bank. This measure will be implemented in the context of a discrete outcome model in the following empirical work.

C. The Construction of Deposit Interest Rates

The second crucial variable in the empirical tests is the deposit interest rate. The empirical work utilizes a proxy for the actual deposit rate paid by individual banks. The preferred choice for the deposit interest rate paid is the rate paid on specific types of deposits at the individual banks in the sample, because these rates would control for different maturities across types of deposits. Instead, the only data obtainable are total interest expenses for all bank deposits at each bank. These data produce an average deposit interest rate for each bank when divided by total deposits at the bank. Therefore, the interest rate used is an average across multiple deposit maturities, and differences in deposit interest rates across banks may reflect different deposit structures among banks.

The theoretical model of Chapter V suggests that the deposit interest rate variable should be measured relative to a risk-constant return on bank assets. Proposition 2 in that chapter demonstrates that it is an increase in the bank's deposit interest rate relative to the bank's average return on investments (for a given risk level) that leads to an increase in bank risk-taking. The empirical model estimated in Chapter VII, then, should incorporate this relationship. To accomplish this, the model includes as an explanatory variable a proxy for a risk-constant asset return; this controls for changes in the asset return, while allowing for examination of the impact of a change in the deposit interest rate on bank riskiness, holding all other influences constant.

Since the proxy for the asset return rate should be risk-constant, I use the return on an essentially risk-free asset, U.S. Treasury bills. This rate must be adjusted so that it allows for the varied maturity times of assets in the bank's asset portfolio; using a convex combination (weighted average) of several annual U.S. Treasury bill rates compensates for the assets' different maturity dates. The Data Appendix describes the determination of these weights. This weighted sum of U.S. Treasury bill rates serves as the proxy in the sample for a risk-constant asset return rate for each year.

Should the deposit interest rate and the asset return rate be measured in nominal or real terms? For an investigation into the impact of bank investments and liabilities on bank failures, nominal interest rates are the relevant choice. Nominal magnitudes define the legal classification of bank failure. That is, in the institutional structure of the banking system, bank contracts are written in nominal terms, and the outcome of these nominal contracts determine whether a bank fails. The government's legal decision to close a bank, moreover, depends on a bank's nominal value.

For banks, nominal rates characterize bank activities through two critical values. First is the return on bank loans. A bank's loans usually are contracted in nominal terms at a fixed rate during the time period under consideration, so that the return on the loan portfolio is affected by changes in inflation rates. An increase in the inflation rate would increase the probability of bankruptcy, then, because of the concurrent decrease in the real return to the bank on its portfolio.[3] A bank with a larger portion of its loans made at fixed nominal rates would be riskier than one with a smaller portion of loans at fixed nominal rates. Secondly, the deposit interest rates paid by banks, as well as the ceilings in effect in the earlier time period, are also denominated in nominal terms. The bank's loan rates are generally fixed for the long-term, but its nominal deposit obligations are short-term, so changes in short-term nominal rates would alter bank profits and the probability of bankruptcy. Since nominal magnitudes demarcate essential values in a bank's activities, they will be used in the empirical tests in the following chapters.

Finally, the regulated time period, 1974-80, poses an possible problem in the measurement of actual deposit interest rates. Under regulation, deposit rate ceilings allowed a maximum explicit interest rate, but banks often provided additional services or reduced service fees as a form of implicit interest on bank deposits. As explained above, calculation of deposit interest rates utilizes only total explicit deposit interest rate expenses. The relevant issue for the empirical work, then, is whether this additional implicit interest is significant, or in other words, whether deposit rate ceilings were binding.

Klein [1974] estimates the "competitive" interest rate on deposits through 1970; this competitive rate accounts for implicit and explicit interest payments. He concludes that since the competitive rate performs better empirically in estimations of the money demand function, it is a better measure of the true deposit rate; therefore, ceilings are not binding. He concedes that the truth probably lies somewhere in between the two extreme assumptions about deposit rate ceilings: Ceilings are neither completely effective nor completely ineffective.

By the mid-1970's, when my data set begins, the effectiveness of deposit ceilings seems to have grown. Primary evidence that banks were constrained by deposit rate ceilings comes from the considerable exodus of funds from banks, or disintermediation, during the decade. The inflation of this time period pushed nominal interest rates much higher than the ceiling on bank deposit rates, and evidently even the added value of the bank services provided to large depositors did not compensate fully for this difference in rates. During this period, banks actively campaigned for a repeal of deposit rate ceilings because of this disintermediation; banks clamored for the opportunity to effectively compete for deposits through changes in the deposit rates they paid. The disintermediation and subsequent calls for removal of the ceilings, then, imply that deposit ceilings were binding during the regulated time period covered by my data set, 1974-80.

Notes

1. Banks file call reports with their supervising federal agency. Chapter II describes the jurisdiction of each agency.

2. Schaefer [1987] suggests that bank regulators should use a similar approach in examining bank risk.

3. This argument is true when the bank does not perfectly forecast inflation rates.

Figure 16

Comparison of Pseudo-Beta and Market Beta
for State-Chartered Banks

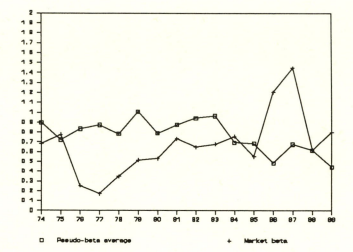

□   Pseudo-beta average   +   Market beta

Figure 17

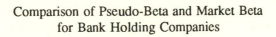

Comparison of Pseudo-Beta and Market Beta
for Bank Holding Companies

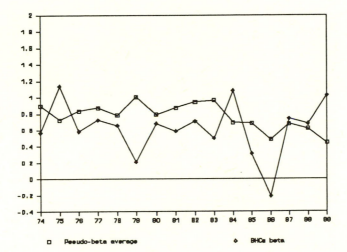

Figure 18

Comparison of Pseudo-Beta and Market Beta
for Hibernia Bank

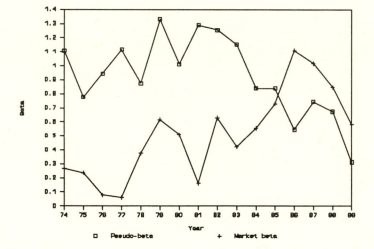

Figure 19

Comparison of Changes in Pseudo-Beta and Market Beta
for Hibernia Bank

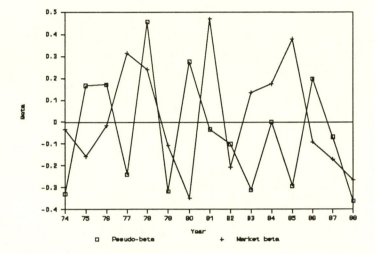

Figure 20

Comparison of Pseudo-Variance and
Market Variance for State-Chartered Banks

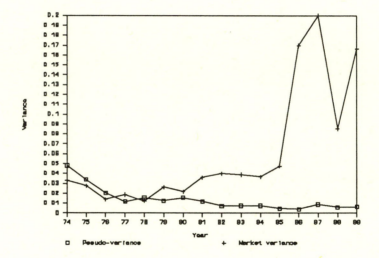

Figure 21

Comparison of Pseudo-Variance and
Market Variance for Bank Holding Companies

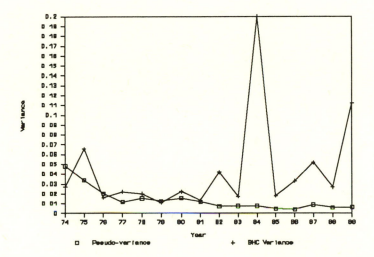

Figure 22

Comparison of Pseudo-Variance and
Market Variance for Hibernia Bank

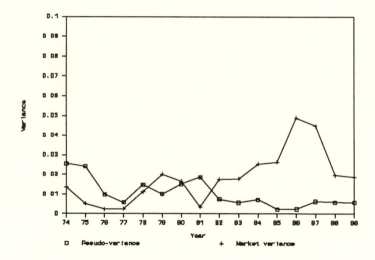

VII. Empirical Evidence on Bank Riskiness

This chapter performs empirical tests of bank risk-taking. As suggested by the model of Chapter V, the empirical work will test whether changes in bank regulation affected the riskiness of bank portfolios by analyzing the relationship between riskiness and interest rates paid on deposits. The first section of this chapter summarizes the data in statistical terms. Next, an empirical model is formulated, based on the theoretical model of Chapter V; this model is estimated using the alternative measures of risk described in the previous chapter. The last two sections extend the simple empirical model to a fixed-effects model, and then to a simultaneous-equations model.

A. Description of the Data

As a first step in examining the impact of deregulation on bank activities, Table 2 and Table 3 present selected summary statistics for the sample. Table 2 provides averages for two sub-periods, the pre-deregulation period of 1974-80, and the deregulation period of 1981-89. Average interest rates are higher under deregulation, providing possible evidence that the deposit rate ceilings were set below the market rate in the regulated period. Risk, as measured by both pseudo-beta and pseudo-variance, is lower in the second period, on average. This may not capture the effect of deregulation on individual bank failures, however, since it averages across both failed and surviving banks and does not control for other influences. Deposits grow more slowly in the second period than in the first. Since it was during the first period that disintermediation escalated, it might be expected that deposits would grow more slowly in that period; in this sample, however, this effect is probably swamped by the growth of the local economy in the first period, and the depression of the economy in the second period. Loans also grow more rapidly in the first period than in the second, again due to the local economic boom in the first period.

Table 3 offers averages by failed- and surviving-bank categories. Both the deposit growth rate and the loan growth rate are greater for failed banks than for non-failed banks; these differences are statistically significant. For failed banks, risk measured by pseudo-beta, is statistically larger; risk proxied by pseudo-variance is not statistically different. This indicates that failed banks were, not surprisingly, riskier than surviving banks. Failed banks also paid somewhat higher average deposit interest rates. Finally, note that failed banks are smaller than surviving banks, in general; this finding is also revealed in some of the following regression results.

B. The Primary Empirical Model

Next, a formal test of the way in which deregulation may influence bank risk-taking is conducted. The model in Chapter V demonstrates that bank portfolio risk increases as deposit interest rates increase, holding all other variables constant. Application of this result to the sample period should incorporate the differences in regulatory structure before and after deregulation. Before deregulation, the model suggests that no strong positive relationship between deposit interest rates and bank risk would exist, because the ceiling on deposit rates imposed similar deposit interest costs on all banks. Because ceilings were different for different types of deposits, the variation in average interest rates paid across banks was due mostly to its deposit mix. Direct regulation of banks, through frequent safety examinations, also served to limit bank riskiness before deregulation. After deregulation, however, as ceilings on deposit interest rates were lifted, some banks took advantage of the opportunity to pay higher deposit interest rates. Banks that paid higher interest rates considered a smaller portion of the risk distribution (less of the downside risk) than banks that paid lower rates, and so chose riskier investments. Also, banks were subject to fewer on-site examinations than before (as illustrated in Chapter II), and this, too, allowed for riskier portfolios.

Then the null hypothesis that the model of Chapter V suggests is this: Deregulation did not affect the relationship between deposit interest rates and bank risk-taking. The alternative hypothesis is that deregulation altered this relationship.

Additional factors should be considered in testing bank risk choices. One such influence is the capital-to-asset ratio for the bank. Kane [1985] holds that financial institutions near insolvency engage in proportionately higher-risk investments, so risk may vary inversely with the bank's capital-to-asset ratio. Other influences on bank riskiness are identified by Gunther [1989], who controls for bank size in his analysis of management risk choices. Bank size may proxy for portfolio diversification, because a larger bank may have more opportunities to diversify, so may be less risky. On the other hand, a larger bank may choose to specialize in a certain category of loans in which it has some expertise, so the larger bank may be relatively less diversified, and more risky, than a smaller bank. In the tests below, I control for the influences of a bank's capital position and size by including the capital-to-asset ratio and total real deposit size, respectively, for each bank.

Economic conditions also play a role in bank riskiness. Intuition suggests that the state of the local economy affects bank riskiness through its impact on bank investments. Furthermore, Eisenbeis [1986] voices the popular opinion that the predominant cause of the recent swell in bank failures is the condition of the local economy. Since the empirical tests in this book strive to investigate this claim, it is vital that some measures of the state of the economy be included in the empirical model. These numbers should be collected at the local level, so that there is variation across banks in the sample. Four possible candidates emerge, each available at the parish (county) level: The unemployment rate, per-capita personal income, new housing units authorized by building permits, and the number of businesses operating. The empirical model specified below includes all four variables. Since the measures are correlated, the estimates of their coefficients may produce large standard errors; this problem will be addressed in the discussion of the empirical results.

Finally, as explained in section VI.C, the theoretical model shows that the empirical model should control for changes in the returns to a risk-constant bank asset. A weighted average of U.S. Treasury bill rates serves as a proxy for this variable.

The appropriate unrestricted model to allow for the impact of deregulation on risk, therefore, evolves from the above discussion as follows:

(1) $$\text{Risk} = a_1 + b_1(\text{interest rate}) + b_2(K/A)$$
$$+ b_3(\text{deposits}) + b_4(\text{dereg})$$
$$+ b_5(\text{dereg*interest rate}) + b_6(\text{t-bill})$$
$$+ b_7(\text{unemployment}) + b_8(\text{houses})$$
$$+ b_9(\text{income}) + b_{10}(\text{businesses}) + e$$

where risk is proxied by one of the measures defined in the previous chapter; interest rate is the deposit interest rate defined in section VI.C; K/A is the capital-to-asset ratio; deposits, which measures bank size, is the total real deposits for the bank; dereg is a dummy variable with the value of one for each year after 1980, and a value of zero otherwise; t-bill is the weighted-average U.S. Treasury bill rate; and the macroeconomic variables, unemployment, housing starts, real personal income per capita, and the number of business establishments, are amounts for the parish in which the bank is located. This specification allows deregulation to alter the influence of deposit interest rates on risk, but constrains the effect of the other independent variables on risk to be the same in both periods, since deregulation is not expected to change those relationships.[1]

1. Results Using Traditional Risk Measures

I first estimate equation (1) with some of the risk measures employed in previous empirical studies. This facilitates comparison of my results using improved definitions of risk, to the performance of traditional measures of risk in the same empirical model. Two risk measures are implemented: the proportion of construction loans, used by Gunther [1989]; and the ratio of net loan charge-offs (loans declared as a loss) to total loans, used by Avery and Hanweck [1984].

The first column of Table 4 reports the estimate of equation (1) with construction loans as the risk measure; the second column, the estimate with net charge-offs as the risk measure. The results differ for the two risk measures. For the former measure, the coefficient on the deposit interest rate is significantly negative during the regulated time period, but for the latter measure, the coefficient is significantly positive. In the deregulated period, the coefficient on the interactive deregulation-deposit interest rate term in the construction-loan regression is positive, but the true coefficient on deposit interest rates remains negative. The deregulation-deposit rate coefficient in the net-charge-offs regression is negative for the deregulated period. In terms of economic significance, both coefficients are small. The simple deregulation dummy variable coefficient is negative for the first regression, but positive for the regression with net charge-offs. Similarly, several other variable coefficients change signs and significance between the two regressions. It is unclear from the results of these two regressions what the true relationship between risk and interest rates might be. Moreover, the discussion of Chapter VI.B.1 demonstrates that risk is not adequately quantified by these traditional measures. In contrast, the alternative measures used below will demonstrate a positive relationship between deposit interest rates and risk after deregulation.

2.   Results Using Pseudo-Beta to Measure Risk

The discussion of part VII.B above indicates that the proper test of the model of Chapter V would be to test for differences in this model between regulated and deregulated time periods, so I begin by estimating equation (1); the regressions use pseudo-beta (defined in section VI.B.1) as the measure of risk. The estimates are presented in the first column of Table 5. The data have been pooled across time and banks over the sample period.[2]

For the deregulated period, 1981-89, the coefficient describing the relationship between interest rates and risk is significantly positive. The coefficient on this interactive interest-rate-deregulation term captures the change in the interest rate coefficient over the two time periods, so the true coefficient on the interest rate in the deregulated time period equals approximately 2.84. This positive relationship is what the model predicts. After deregulation, some banks paid higher interest rates and encountered fewer examinations, so they would have considered less of the downside risk; therefore, they chose riskier investments. On the other hand, the coefficient on the interest rate is significantly negatively related to the pseudo-beta measure of risk in the regulated time period, when the model indicates no strong relationship would exist. Since differences in deposit interest rates during this period arise from variations in bank liability structure, this estimated coefficient implies that deposit structures that induce higher total interest expenses are negatively related to the bank portfolio's total risk during the regulated time period.[3]

The coefficient of the capital-to-asset ratio is positive for the estimate of equation (1). This may result from the measure of the capital-to-asset ratio; my data set contains the book value of capital instead of the market value of capital, which would be the more relevant measure of capital. Because banks have some discretion in accounting procedures, the book value may not reflect the true value of bank capital. Some unobserved adjustment factor relates the book value and the (perhaps substantially different) market value. A higher adjustment factor (or a decrease in the book value to align it more closely with the market value) would be positively related to risk. The positive coefficient, then, may be a measure of connection between the adjustment factor and risk.[4]

The coefficient for the effect of bank size on bank riskiness is significantly positive. This suggests that a larger bank does not necessarily take advantage of more opportunities to diversify, but may instead choose to concentrate its investments in a particular area. Also, the sign of the simple deregulation dummy coefficient is significantly negative, which simply captures the decrease in the intercept term in the second period. The coefficient on U.S. Treasury bill rates, which proxies the bank's return on a risk-constant asset, is positive, signifying that an increase in bank asset returns for a given risk level increases bank riskiness.

The remaining variables constitute the effects of the local economy. The coefficient on the unemployment rate is negative, so a downturn in the economy, proxied by an increase in the unemployment rate, corresponds to a decrease in bank risk-taking. Similarly, the positive coefficient on housing starts suggests the same relationship between the local economy and risk. The estimates of the coefficients on per-capita real personal income and total businesses denote the opposite relationship, but both coefficients are statistically insignificant. The direct correspondence between the local economy and riskiness suggested by these estimates may arise because a bank responds to a weaker economy by loaning less than before in an effort to protect the bank from the downturn, and so is inclined to take on less-risky investments than before. It may also be that the bank faces fewer opportunities to loan money when the economy slows.

Since multicollinearity may lead to high standard errors for this group of variables, individual t-tests of the coefficients' significance are unreliable; instead, an F-test evaluates the joint significance of these variables. The null hypothesis for the test maintains that $b_7=b_8=b_9=b_{10}=0$ in equation (1). The model of equation (2), below, constrains the macroeconomic coefficients to be zero; the F-test compares it to the unconstrained model, equation (1). The constrained model for the local economic variables, then, is

$$
(2) \qquad \text{Risk} = a_1 + b_1(\text{interest rate}) + b_2(K/A)
$$
$$
+ b_3(\text{deposits}) + b_4(\text{dereg})
$$
$$
+ b_5(\text{dereg*interest rate}) + b_6(\text{t-bill})
$$
$$
+ e
$$

Column 2 of Table 5 displays the estimate of equation (2). The F value is 50.84, which indicates that the local-economy variable coefficients as a group are significantly different from zero.[5]

Finally, while the t-tests show that the individual coefficients on deregulation are significantly different from zero, the combined significance of the deregulation effects should also be examined. An F-test of the significance of this regime change is performed next. The F-test considers the joint null hypothesis that $b_4=b_5=0$ in equation (1); that is, it measures the combined significance of the changes due to deregulation. The unconstrained model is equation (1), while the constrained model is as follows:

$$
(3) \qquad \text{Risk} = a_1 + b_1(\text{interest rate}) + b_2(K/A)
$$
$$
+ b_3(\text{deposits}) + b_4(\text{t-bill})
$$
$$
+ b_5(\text{unemployment}) + b_6(\text{houses})
$$
$$
+ b_7(\text{income}) + b_8(\text{businesses}) + e
$$

Equation (3) is estimated using the same pooled data set over the full time period, and the results are presented in the third column of Table 5. The coefficient describing the impact of deposit interest rates on risk is positive but statistically insignificant for the full sample. The coefficient of the capital-to-asset ratio is again insignificantly different from zero, although its sign is now negative; the coefficients on the remaining variables retain the same qualitative relationships to risk as before. Using the restricted model of equation (3) and the unrestricted model of equation (1), the computed F-statistic is 80.41, which shows that the coefficients jointly are significant at the one percent level,[6] so the null hypothesis that deregulation did not affect riskiness is rejected.

Once estimated, the model in Table 5 facilitates some insights into the economic significance of the risk relationship. Deposit interest rates demonstrate a significant influence on risk in the deregulated time period. The coefficient on deposit rates is about 2.85, so an increase of 0.01 in the interest rate, from 0.05 to 0.06, for example, increases risk by about four percent.[7] Moving from the first quartile to the third quartile value of the deposit interest rate increases risk by approximately eleven percent. For the capital-to-asset ratio, a five percent increase results in a one percent growth in risk, which is rather small; furthermore, the move from the first quartile value to the third produces an increase of only 0.7 percent. Bank size demonstrates a minor impact on bank portfolio risk: the change from the first to third quartile value induces a 0.8 percent climb in pseudo-beta. As an example of the influence of local economic conditions, consider the estimate for the unemployment rate coefficient. The range between the first and third quartile leads to a five percent decrease in the pseudo-beta, a moderate change.

3. Results Using Pseudo-Variance to Measure Risk

The previous sub-section employed pseudo-beta as the measure of risk in examining the impact on bank risk of deposit interest rate deregulation. This sub-section considers a different risk variable which encompasses total risk as well as systematic risk, the pseudo-variance of bank portfolio returns. (Calculation of this variance is described in Section VI.B.2.)

For comparison, the same set of regressions estimated for the pseudo-beta also will be estimated for the pseudo-variance. The first results, in column one of Table 6, use pseudo-variance as the measure of risk and estimate equation (1). The coefficient on deposit interest rates is significant and positive for the deregulated period. This is what the model predicts, since it demonstrates that an increase in the interest rate paid on deposits leads to an increased likelihood of bank failure, which is measured by the bank's portfolio variance. The coefficient on this interactive interest-rate-deregulation term measures the change in the interest rate coefficient after deregulation, so the true coefficient on the interest rate in the deregulated time period equals approximately 0.03. However, in the regulated period, the coefficient on the interest rate is significantly negatively related to risk as measured by pseudo-variance; as before, this may reflect the different liability maturities of different banks.

The coefficient describing the relationship between the capital-to-asset ratio and total risk shifts to insignificance, although it now acquires the expected negative sign. The simple deregulation dummy variable coefficient retains the negative relation to risk established in Table 5. The coefficient on bank deposits, the proxy for bank size, is now negative; while larger banks may choose higher systematic risk than smaller banks, they display less vulnerability to total risk. The coefficient on the proxy for risk-constant bank asset returns remains positive, but loses its statistical significance.

Using total risk also transforms the signs on two of the macroeconomic variable coefficients, housing starts and businesses in operation; furthermore, the coefficient on businesses becomes statistically significant, while that on housing loses its significance.[8] The coefficients offer no unified insight into the qualitative relationship between the local economy and total risk, because two suggest a positive relationship, while the other two signal the opposite. The second column of Table 6 reports the estimate of the constrained regression (2). The combined impact of the macroeconomic variables persists: An F-test of the constrained regression with the unconstrained regression (1) produces an F-statistic of 5.53, which suggests that the coefficients are jointly significantly different from zero at the one-percent level.

A second F-test evaluates the overall significance of the impact of deregulation on total risk. The third column of Table 6 summarizes the estimate of equation (3); the variable coefficients maintain qualitative relationships with total risk analogous to those reported in the first column. The F-statistic of 58.00 establishes that the null hypothesis that the deregulation coefficients jointly equal zero can be rejected at the one-percent level of significance.

Consider now the economic significance of the coefficient estimates. Under deregulation, the coefficient on deposit interest rates reveals that an increase by 0.01 in this variable value elicits a two-and-one-half percent increase in pseudo-variance. Moving from the first quartile value of deposit rates to the third brings about a seven percent increase in pseudo-variance. Deposit interest rates affect pseudo-variance, then, on a somewhat smaller scale than with pseudo-beta. The economic importance of the capital-to-asset ratio and bank size coefficients remain modest when risk is defined by pseudo-variance; the first-to-third- quartile range in each variable accounts for a 1.2 percent decrease in risk. Finally, the coefficient on unemployment illustrates that the relation between the local economy and risk expands somewhat: as unemployment moves from its first-quartile value to its third-quartile value, pseudo-variance falls by approximately eight percent.

In sum, with pseudo-variance as the measure of risk, the empirical evidence on the risk-interest rate relationship indicates a positive relationship for the deregulated time period, and rejects the null hypothesis that no change occurred in this relationship after deregulation. Evidence from the pseudo-variance model, however, offers conflicting stories about the impact of the local economy. In comparison to the pseudo-beta model, the economic significance of the coefficient on deposit interest rates declines slightly, while the others retain roles similar to those found in the pseudo-beta regression. The empirical tests using pseudo-variance, then, support the primary conclusion drawn from the pseudo-beta test--that interest rates and risk are positively related under deregulation.

4.   Results Using the Probability of Failure to Measure Risk

Regressions in this sub-section incorporate a third proxy measure of risk, the eventual failure or survival of the individual bank. This variable encompasses total risk for a bank (systematic and unsystematic) by considering the discrete outcome of each bank's behavior: failure or survival. If a bank fails at some point in the given period, its status is one; otherwise, its status is zero.

Using this alternate measure of risk, I first test for the influence of the deregulation of nominal deposit interest rates on risk by estimating a probit version of equation (1). The first column of Table 7 relates the results of this regression. The coefficient on deposit interest rates is negatively related to this measure of risk in the regulated time period, but is statistically insignificant. The applied model predicts this relationship; also, since only two banks failed during the regulated time period of the sample, this result is not surprising. In the deregulated time period, the deposit-interest-rate coefficient holds a positive relationship to this measure of bank riskiness, as the earlier regressions also demonstrated for the other measures; the coefficient on the deposit interest rate becomes approximately 15.87.

The simple deregulation dummy variable coefficient loses its significance in this regression, indicating no shift in the intercept between the two periods. The coefficient of the capital-to-asset ratio now takes the expected negative sign, and is significantly different from zero. The coefficient on bank size reverses sign from the pseudo-beta estimates; it is now significantly negatively related to the probability of failure. This may be a reflection of the fact that the FDIC considers bank size in its decision to declare a bank failed. (Some banks are considered "too big to fail," for instance.) The coefficient on the proxy for bank asset returns is insignificantly different from zero.

The local-economy variable coefficients reveal a positive relation between risk and the state of the economy, as they also do for the pseudo-beta risk measure, although the statistical significance of the coefficients switch. As usual, the second column of the table recounts the estimates of the constrained equation, which tests for the joint significance of these variable coefficients. Since these are probit models, the likelihood ratio (LR) test, instead of the F-test, now yields a test statistic for the null hypothesis that the combined significance of the macroeconomic variable coefficients equals zero. The LR value is 379.49, which confirms that the joint influence of these variables is significantly different from zero.[9]

Next, the third column of Table 7 describes the estimate of equation (3), which constrains the coefficients on deregulation and the deregulation interactive term to equal zero. The LR test statistic, 85.92, rejects the null hypothesis that total impact on deregulation is equal to zero.[10] This conclusion is consistent with that drawn from the other two risk measures, as well.

Lastly, Table 8 illustrates the economic importance of several variables in the estimated model. Calibrated values of the coefficients in probit models do not represent partial derivatives, as they do in an OLS model; nor are the partial derivatives constant in a probit model. Instead, since the partial derivatives change with the values of the explanatory variables, they are calculated at points corresponding to the five quartile values of each variable.[11] Under deregulation, at the median value of the deposit interest rate, the partial derivative for this variable coefficient is 1.78; an increase in the interest rate of 0.01 increases the probability of failure by about two percent, assuming other variables are held constant. The change in the interquartile range increases the probability of failure by twenty-one percent, a substantial amount. For the capital-to-asset ratio, the interquartile increase induces a small 0.3 percent decrease in the probability of failure. For bank size (total deposits), the change between the first- and third-quartile values corresponds to a 0.5 percent decline in the probability of failure. Finally, the same interquartile increase in the unemployment rate decreases the probability of failure by a small 0.2 percent. The impact of the remaining local-economy coefficients varies from a one percent increase for the number of businesses to a 0.09 percent increase for housing starts, assuming the usual interquartile changes. Each estimate is small relative to the estimated impact of a change in deposit interest rates.

Overall, the empirical results using bank status as a measure of total risk indicate that deposit interest rates exert a positive influence on bank riskiness after deregulation, and no strong influence before deregulation; these results support the theoretical model predictions. Defining total risk as bank status yields empirical estimates comparable to those obtained using both the pseudo-beta and pseudo-variance as the measure of total risk, since both suggest a positive relationship for deposit interest rates in the deregulated period.

C. The Fixed-Effects Model

The primary empirical model developed in Section VII.B assumes that the parameter coefficients for each bank are the same; it allows for no individual differences in coefficients among the banks in the sample. It is possible, instead, that certain parameter coefficients vary across banks. For example, some unique characteristic that is not captured by the variables already in the model may be included in the intercept term, so its coefficient would vary across banks. This section explicitly models the possibility that individual bank coefficient values differ by exploiting the additional information that a panel data set provides, and investigates the impact of that assumption on the empirical results.

The model to be constructed here assumes that each bank in the data set possesses some unique characteristic which is not directly observable. One likely attribute that varies across banks is management skill or technique; individual banks procure different management-skill levels depending on the individual managers hired.[12] Since this factor is difficult to quantify, it has not been included in the model so far. The exclusion of a relevant explanatory variable introduces bias in the empirical estimates of the coefficients and their standard errors. However, a fixed-effects model accommodates the inclusion of such an otherwise-unobservable individual factor, and therefore provides estimates of the model coefficients which control for the systematic heterogeneity of banks.

How is this concept integrated into the empirical model? Hsiao [1986] shows that regression-based models can be transformed easily to accommodate the individual-bank fixed effect. The transformation utilized here involves calculating the mean of each variable for each bank, then subtracting the bank's mean value of each variable from each of its observations; these altered observations make up the new data set for a simple OLS regression.[13] This deviation-from-within-group-means process removes the individual bank effects embedded in each observation.

The estimate of this fixed-effect model, using pseudo-beta as the risk measure, comprises Table 9.[14] All values are expressed as deviations from within-group means. In the regulated time period, the significantly negative coefficient between deposit interest rates and risk remains; under deregulation, the positive and significant coefficient also persists. This latter result supports the empirical model's predictions and the earlier tests with pseudo-beta (Table 5). The capital-to-asset ratio coefficient resumes the positive sign of the earlier pseudo-beta regression, as well. The coefficient on bank deposits becomes negative and is now significant at the five-percent level. The set of coefficients on the macroeconomic variables show few qualitative changes between the fixed-effect model and the simple model: the coefficient on personal income becomes positive, but is still insignificant; and the coefficient on businesses operating becomes significant, but is still negative. The familiar F-test of their joint importance (which produces an F-statistic equal to 550.51) rejects the null hypothesis that the coefficients jointly equal zero.[15]

Table 10 summarizes the fixed-effects model when pseudo-variance is used as the risk measure. In this case, the fixed-effects model displays somewhat altered results compared to the basic empirical model (Table 6). While the negative relationship between interest rates and risk in the regulated period that occurred in the basic model does not fade in this model, the previously significant and positive coefficient on deposit interest rates in the deregulated time period loses its statistical significance in the fixed-effects model. Moreover, the adjusted coefficient for this period becomes negative, -0.0822. The coefficient on total deposits loses its significance, as well. The local-economy variable coefficients retain their combined significance, certified by an F-statistic of 267.36.

The basic empirical model also utilizes a third risk measure, bank status, in its estimates. No fixed-effects model is estimated for this risk measure, because the maximum-likelihood method used in estimating the basic probit model cannot readily be extended to a fixed-effects model. This limitation arises from the relationship between estimators in the probit model. Estimators of the individual fixed effects, or individual intercept terms, are inconsistent when the time period involved is small, as in this data set. In the probit model, the maximum-likelihood estimators of the common (slope) coefficients depend on estimates of the intercept terms, so the slope coefficients also will be inconsistent. (Hsiao [1986], page 159, discusses this point in more detail.)

In sum, then, incorporating individual bank effects into the primary empirical model does not significantly alter the previous empirical results when the risk measure is pseudo-beta. When risk is measured instead with pseudo-variance, the previously-estimated positive relationship between interest rates and risk under deregulation disappears; instead, these variables display no significant relationship in the deregulated period.

D. A Model Incorporating Simultaneity

In the above empirical tests, the empirical model postulates that deposit interest rates are an independent explanatory variable in the model. Because that is a restrictive assumption, this section turns to a model that allows risk to influence deposit interest rates at the same time that deposit interest rates affect risk. First comes a discussion of the possible forces that create the simultaneity. The next paragraphs define the simultaneous model and determine if it can be formally identified. Once the model has been identified through specific exclusion restrictions, it is estimated using the pseudo-beta and pseudo-variance risk measures.

The empirical model investigated in the preceding sections assumes that the interest rate is the independent variable and risk is the dependent variable. It may be that causality occurs in the other direction, as well. That is, a bank which chooses to take more risks in its investments may also wish to compete more aggressively for deposits, so the bank pays higher deposit interest rates to attract more deposits. In particular, the connection may be especially acute for problem banks: A bank that is close to failure may attempt to grow out of its problems with an aggressive deposit rate stance, so that portfolio riskiness influences deposit interest rates, as deposit interest rates simultaneously affect riskiness. Addressing this possibility requires a simultaneous-equations model of the mutual dependence of risk and deposit interest rates.

The simultaneous model consists of equation (1), representing the determinants of risk, and a new equation, below, characterizing the components of the deposit interest rate relationship. This model introduces an additional explanatory variable, the market deposit rate. The model specifies that market rates help determine bank deposit rates; banks face a competitively-determined market deposit interest rate. Additionally, bank size, as proxied by total bank deposits, drops out of this equation, since it is not obvious that bank size should affect the deposit rate paid. Given these restrictions, the interest-rate equation can be written as

$$
\begin{aligned}
(4) \quad \text{Interest rate} = {} & a_2 + b_{11}(\text{risk}) + b_{12}(\text{K/A}) \\
& + b_{13}(\text{dereg}) + b_{14}(\text{dereg*risk}) \\
& + b_{15}(\text{mkt. rate}) + b_{16}(\text{unemployment}) \\
& + b_{17}(\text{houses}) + b_{18}(\text{income}) \\
& + b_{19}(\text{businesses}) + e
\end{aligned}
$$

where "mkt. rate" is the market deposit interest rate, and the other variables remain as before. This model fulfills the order condition for identification, since each equation excludes one exogenous variable; it also satisfies the rank condition.

Since the model can be identified, it is estimated using the two-stage least squares (2SLS) method. A proxy for the market rate of interest should reflect the market for bank deposits, so I employ the secondary-market rate on certificates of deposit with a three-month maturity. Finally, the simultaneous model utilizes pseudo-beta and pseudo-variance as the risk measures.

1. Results Using Pseudo-Beta to Measure Risk

Table 11 contains the results from the 2SLS estimation of equation (1) when risk is measured by pseudo-beta. The estimated coefficients of equation (1), accounting for simultaneity, differ in several ways. Most importantly, the coefficient describing the relationship between deposit interest rates and bank risk under regulation becomes positive and statistically significant. This result reflects the spirit of the model more than the earlier results, but it is not inconsistent with the empirical model estimated earlier. In both cases, the primary concern is whether the interest rate-risk relation changed with deregulation. The null hypothesis specified in Section VII.B states that no change in this relationship occurred, while the alternative hypothesis maintains that the relationship grew more important. Both the 2SLS estimate and the basic model estimate indicate that the connection did become more important.

Additionally, the simultaneous-equation model transforms some of the macroeconomic variable coefficients. The coefficients on both real personal income and the number of businesses in operation become positive, so the coefficients on the macroeconomic variables now present a cohesive view of their impact on bank risk in the simultaneous-equations model. Each of the macroeconomic-variable coefficients now predicts an increase in bank risk-taking with an upturn in economic activity.

Lastly, the coefficient on the proxy for bank asset returns, the weightedaverage of U.S. Treasury bill rates, switches to negative. The remaining variable coefficients in equation (1) reflect relationships to risk that are generally similar to those estimated in the basic model using pseudo-beta (Table 5).

The economic importance of the interest rate-risk relationship swells in the simultaneous model. A small one-percent rise in interest rates in the deregulated time period now yields an eleven-percent increase in the pseudo-beta measure of risk. As for the other variable coefficients, total deposits and the local-economy coefficients retain a qualitatively similar relation to risk as before, in Table 5. The capital-to-asset ratio coefficient becomes statistically significant, although its economic impact remains small: a ten-percent hike in the ratio yields a 0.12 percent increase in riskiness. The estimate of the risk equation in the simultaneous model, then, generally confirms the primary findings of the basic model.

Table 11 also states the 2SLS estimates of the coefficients for the interest-rate equation (4). The coefficient on risk, measured by pseudo-beta, is insignificant in the regulated time period, but negatively related to deposit interest rates in the deregulated period. This puzzling result may arise because of an omitted-variable bias in the deposit interest rate equation. One important variable that has been excluded from the equation is the bank management skill level. More skilled management may conduct sophisticated "liability management" techniques, in which liability maturities are closely matched to asset maturities; this increased skill may imply a lower average deposit interest rate. While quantitative data on skill levels at individual banks are assembled by bank examiners, the data are not publicly available, so cannot be included in this study.

The capital-to-asset ratio coefficient shows a negative relationship to interest rates, as expected. The coefficient for the certificate of deposit rate also displays its expected positive sign, as does the simple deregulation dummy variable. The coefficients on unemployment, per-capita income, and numbers of businesses operating imply an inverse relation between economic upswings and the interest rate; the coefficient on housing starts suggests the opposite. These differences may arise because the local-economy variables proxy the state of the economy with differing lag times; housing starts reflect an economic upturn before the other variables do.

Overall, the simultaneous model estimated here offers evidence supportive of the hypothesis that the risk-interest rate relationship was more strongly positive under deregulation. The coefficients of deposit interest rates are both significantly positive, while the other coefficients retain their qualitative relationships from the single-equation model. The coefficients of the interest rate equation, though, produce counter-intuitive results about its relationship to risk; this equation may suffer from an omitted-variable bias.

2.   Results Using Pseudo-Variance to Measure Risk

Table 12 reports the 2SLS estimate of equation (1), the risk equation, when pseudo-variance is implemented to measure bank riskiness. As in the basic model, the coefficient on deposit interest rates is negative for the regulated time period. The coefficient on the interactive deregulation-interest rate term remains positive and significant, but the true coefficient for this period (the sum of the coefficient from the first period and the second period) becomes negative, since it now equals -0.60. This confirms that the risk-deposit rate relationship shifted significantly after deregulation, so it is not incompatible with the stated alternative hypothesis; but the result is inconsistent with the prediction of the theoretical model, namely, that an increase in deposit rates leads to an increase in bank risk-taking.

Of the remaining coefficients, only the signs on the macroeconomic variable coefficients deviate in the simultaneous-equation model. The coefficients on the measures of local economic activity provide conflicting evidence about the economy's influence on bank riskiness. The unemployment coefficient becomes positive, implying that an upturn in the economy leads to an upturn in bank risk; the coefficient on businesses operating also signals this relation. The coefficients on the other two local-economy variables, however, suggest a negative relation between economic activity and bank risk.

The second column of Table 12 displays the 2SLS estimate of equation (4), the interest rate equation, when the risk measure is pseudo-variance. In this regression, risk and deposit interest rates exhibit the positive relationship that the theoretical model predicts; however, the change in this relation after deregulation is not statistically significant. The other coefficient estimates resemble those of the estimated 2SLS interest-rate equation using pseudo-beta as the measure of risk.

Use of pseudo-variance in the simultaneous-equation model, then, generates mixed implications about the effect of deregulation on the interest rate-risk relation. The interest-rate equation indicates a positive relation that did not change, while the risk equation suggests a negative relation that became significantly less negative after deregulation. The ambiguity of these results may stem from the risk measure utilized. Pseudo-variance contains more "noise" than pseudo-beta, since the former includes unsystematic risk as well as systematic risk. This introduces additional movement in pseudo-variance which may not be directly connected to actual bank experience. While both measures rely on equity-market data in computing bank risk, the lack of direct connection to actual bank experience would be exaggerated with pseudo-variance, and this divergence between bank portfolio risk and pseudo-variance may distort the regression estimates.

Notes

1. The model predicts changes only in the interest rate coefficient, and the 1980 deregulation directly affects only the interest rate variable coefficient. Regressions not reported here suggest the other coefficients do not change.

2. The low R-squared statistics are not surprising for cross-section time-series data.

3. When equation (1) is estimated as part of a simultaneous-equations model in part VII.D, this negative relationship disappears. This suggests that the negative interest rate coefficient reported here suffers from simultaneity bias.

4. Tests indicate that both heteroskedasticity and serial correlation are present in these estimates. Wooldridge [1989] proposes a method that corrects for both of these problems. As an approximation, I instead utilize the White [1980] heteroskedasticity adjustment to standard errors; this eliminates the statistical significance on the coefficient of the capital-to-asset ratio.

5. At the one-percent level of significance, the critical value for this F-test 3.32.

6. The critical value of F at the one-percent level for this test is 4.61.

7. All percentages are calculated relative to the sample median value of the variable.

8. The White [1980] adjustment to the standard errors eliminates the statistical significance of the coefficient on real personal income, so that only two of the macroeconomic variable coefficients are statistically significant.

9. The LR statistic is distributed as chi-squared; the critical value at the one-percent level of significance with four degrees of freedom equals 13.28.

10. At the one-percent significance level, the chi-squared critical value with two degrees of freedom is 9.21.

11. These calculations assume that the other variable values are at their respective medians.

12. Alternatively, it might be postulated that management objectives vary across banks. This alternative assumption is equally compatible with the model derived in this section.

13. An alternate method of estimation would be to include in the empirical model a simple dummy variable for each bank in the sample.

14. The reported standard errors are corrected for the additional degrees of freedom taken by the estimations of individual bank means.

15. Since the fixed-effect transformation of the model drops the intercept term, no test of the joint significance of the coefficients of the simple deregulation variable and interactive deregulation-interest rate term is reported.

Table 2

Selected Averages for Louisiana Banks,
Pre- and Post-Deregulation

Variable	1974-80	1981-89	1974-89
Bank portfolio risk (pseudo-beta)[a]	0.843 (0.174)[b]	0.713[c] (0.253)	0.768 (0.232)
Bank portfolio risk (pseudo-variance)[a]	0.022 (0.018)	0.007[c] (0.014)	0.013 (0.018)
Average interest rate paid on deposits	0.038 (0.012)	0.064[c] (0.015)	0.053 (0.019)
Capital-to-asset ratio	0.085 (0.030)	0.096[c] (0.047)	0.092 (0.041)
Real deposits (millions)	0.086 (0.175)	0.096 (0.237)	0.092 (0.213)
Weighted average of U.S. Treasury bill rates	0.069 (0.018)	0.085[c] (0.011)	0.078 (0.016)
Unemployment rate	0.073 (0.019)	0.117[c] (0.029)	0.100 (0.040)
Established businesses (thousands)	2.069 (2.831)	2.655[c] (3.501)	2.395 (3.234)
Real income per-capita (thousands)	7.893 (1.792)	9.142[c] (1.789)	8.589 (1.895)
Housing starts (thousands)	0.800 (1.423)	0.542[c] (1.100)	0.644 (1.244)
Deposit growth rate (real)	0.093 (0.373)	0.053[c] (0.375)	0.069 (0.375)

Loan growth rate (real)	0.103 (0.585)	0.054 (0.490)	0.069 (0.520)

[a]Pseudo-beta and pseudo-variance are defined in section VI.B.1 and section VI.B.2, respectively.
[b]Standard deviations are in parentheses.
[c]The difference between the means in the two periods is significantly different from zero at the one-percent level.

Table 3

Selected Averages for Louisiana Banks,
by Failed and Surviving Bank Categories

Variable	Non-failed Banks	Failed Banks
Bank portfolio risk (pseudo-beta)[a]	0.758 (0.231)[b]	0.834[c] (0.229)
Bank portfolio risk (pseudo-variance)[a]	0.014 (0.018)	0.007[c] (0.004)
Average interest rate paid on deposits	0.052 (0.018)	0.057[c] (0.020)
Capital-to-asset ratio	0.093 (0.038)	0.085[c] (0.054)
Real deposits (millions)	0.096 (0.228)	0.066[c] (0.082)
Weighted average of U.S. Treasury bill rates	0.078 (0.016)	0.086[c] (0.011)
Unemployment rate	0.101 (0.040)	0.095[c] (0.037)
Businesses established (thousands)	2.219 (3.116)	3.340[c] (3.682)
Real income per-capita (thousands)	8.500 (1.830)	9.097[c] (2.161)
Housing starts (thousands)	0.584 (1.190)	1.002[c] (1.478)
Real deposit growth rate	0.036 (0.091)	0.051[c] (0.121)
Real loan growth rate	0.019 (0.100)	0.046[c] (0.155)

See Table 2 for notes.

Table 4

Estimate of the Impact of Deposit Interest Rates on Bank Riskiness

Dependent Variable: Bank loan portfolio risk, measured by the proportion of construction loans, Column 1; and net charge-offs, Column 2[a]

Independent Variable	*Column 1*	*Column 2*
Intercept	-0.0212[c]	0.0135[c]
	(0.0101)	(0.0021)[b]
Average interest rate paid on deposits	-0.7466[c]	0.0668[c]
	(0.1613)	(0.0322)
Capital-to-asset ratio	-0.0005	-0.0004[c]
	(0.0003)	(0.0001)
Real deposits (in millions)	0.0208[c]	-0.0002
	(0.0052)	(0.0011)
Deregulation	-0.0356[c]	0.0200[c]
	(0.0093)	(0.0019)
Average interest rate * deregulation	0.5917[c]	-0.2466[c]
	(0.1672)	(0.0343)
U.S. Treasury bill rate	0.4134[c]	-0.1009[c]
	(0.0848)	(0.0182)
Unemployment	-0.0004	0.0003[c]
	(0.0004)	(0.0001)
Housing starts	0.0085[c]	-0.0011[c]
	(0.0011)	(0.0002)
Real per-capita income	0.0091[c]	0.0003
	(0.0009)	(0.0002)
Businesses	-0.0028[c]	0.0002[c]
	(0.0005)	(0.0001)

Number of observations	3224	3501
Adjusted R-squared	0.1281	0.1174

[a]Section VII.B.2. describes these risk measures.
[b]Standard errors are in parentheses below coefficients.
[c]Coefficient is significantly different from zero at the five-percent level.

Table 5

Estimate of the Impact of Deposit Interest Rates
on Bank Riskiness

Dependent Variable: Bank loan portfolio risk, measured by pseudo-beta[a]

Independent Variable	Equation 1	Equation 2	Equation 3
Intercept	0.7828[c] (0.0341)[b]	0.7260[c] (0.0219)	0.9376[c] (0.0271)
Average interest rate paid on deposits	-1.8281[c] (0.5171)	-2.6533[c] (0.5241)	0.0598 (0.2857)
Capital-to-asset ratio	0.0019[c] (0.0009)	0.0013[c] (0.0009)	0.0006 (0.0009)
Real deposits (in millions)	0.1302[c] (0.0177)	0.1784[c] (0.0166)	0.1349[c] (0.0181)
Deregulation	-0.3607[c] (0.0311)	-0.4206[c] (0.0281)	
Average interest rate * deregulation	4.6730[c] (0.5522)	5.0218[c] (0.5513)	
U.S. Treasury bill rate	2.2698[c] (0.2914)	2.9384[c] (0.2922)	1.8301[c] (0.2883)
Unemployment	-0.0087[c] (0.0013)		-0.0177[c] (0.0010)
Housing starts	0.0270[c] (0.0037)		0.0340[c] (0.0038)
Real per-capita income	-0.0001 (0.0033)		-0.0164[c] (0.0030)
Businesses	-0.0002 (0.0018)		-0.0014 (0.0018)

Number of observations	3501	3501	3501
Adjusted R-squared	0.1980	0.1522	0.1615

[a]Pseudo-beta is defined in Section VI.B.1.
[b]Standard errors are in parentheses below coefficients.
[c]Coefficient is significantly different from zero at the five-percent level.

Table 6

Estimate of the Impact of Deposit Interest Rates on Bank Riskiness

Dependent Variable: Bank loan portfolio risk, measured by pseudo-variance[a]

Independent Variable	Equation 1	Equation 2	Equation 3
Intercept	0.0336[c] (0.0027)[b]	0.0271[c] (0.0017)	0.0473[c] (0.0022)
Average interest rate paid on deposits	-0.2018[c] (0.0416)	-0.2194[c] (0.0411)	-0.1531[c] (0.0023)
Capital-to-asset ratio	-0.0001 (0.0001)	-0.0001 (0.0001)	-0.0003[c] (0.0001)
Real deposits (in millions)	-0.0034[c] (0.0014)	-0.0017 (0.0013)	-0.0031[c] (0.0014)
Deregulation	-0.0217[c] (0.0025)	-0.0232[c] (0.0022)	
Average interest rate * deregulation	0.2340[c] (0.0445)	0.2412[c] (0.0433)	
U.S. Treasury bill rate	0.0319 (0.0235)	0.0319 (0.0229)	0.0149 (0.0231)
Unemployment	-0.0002[c] (0.0001)		-0.0009[c] (0.0001)
Housing starts	-0.0006[d] (0.0003)		-0.0001 (0.0003)
Real per-capita income	-0.0007[c] (0.0003)		-0.0020[c] (0.0002)
Businesses	0.0006[c] (0.0001)		0.0005[c] (0.0001)

Number of observations	3501	3501	3501
Adjusted R-squared	0.1443	0.1399	0.1164

[a]Pseudo-variance is defined in Section VI.B.2.
[b]Standard errors are in parentheses below coefficients.
[c]Coefficient is significantly different from zero at the five-percent level.
[d]Coefficient is significantly different from zero at the ten-percent level.

Table 7

Estimate of the Impact of Deposit Interest Rates on Bank Riskiness

Dependent Variable: Bank status, equal to one if the bank fails in the sample period, and zero otherwise[a]

Independent Variable	Equation 1	Equation 2	Equation 3
Intercept	-3.0885[c] (0.6373)[b]	-2.2350[c] (0.4782)	-5.2886[c] (0.3906)
Average interest rate paid on deposits	-7.3762 (13.3798)	-5.9714 (12.0401)	24.9677[c] (2.8502)
Capital-to-asset ratio	-0.0187[c] (0.0084)	-0.0210[c] (0.0079)	-0.0046 (0.0081)
Real deposits (in millions)	-1.9000[c] (0.3541)	-0.5581[c] (0.2491)	-1.8700[c] (0.3436)
Deregulation	0.4915 (0.5642)	0.80501[d] (0.4798)	
Average interest rate * deregulation	23.2502[d] (13.3875)	16.8827 (12.0456)	
U.S. Treasury bill rate	-3.5925 (3.8356)	-1.3031 (3.2735)	-1.0149 (3.3826)
Unemployment	-0.0043 (0.0127)		0.0512[c] (0.0102)
Housing starts	0.0224 (0.0347)		-0.0147 (0.0328)
Real per-capita income	0.1063[c] (0.0341)		0.2146[c] (0.0301)
Businesses	-0.0677[c] (0.0152)		0.0645[c] (0.0146)

Number of observations	3502	4278	3502
Likelihood Ratio statistic	500.7[c]	413.9[c]	414.8[c]

[a]Bank status is defined in Section VI.B.3.
[b]Standard errors are in parentheses below coefficients.
[c]The coefficient is significantly different from zero at the five-percent level.
[d]The coefficient is significant at the ten-percent level.

Table 8

Estimates of the Partial Derivatives
of Explanatory Variables on Bank Riskiness

Dependent Variable: Bank status, equal to one if the bank fails in the sample period, and zero otherwise[a]

Independent Variable	Q0	Q1	Q2	Q3	Q4
Average interest rate * dereg	0.1023	0.1023	1.7763	3.2573	11.3460
Capital-to-asset ratio	-0.0023	-0.0014	-0.0014	-0.0013	0.0
Real deposits	-0.1651	-0.1535	-0.1452	-0.1294	-0.0002
U.S. Treasury bill rate	-0.3416	-0.2957	-0.2745	-0.2543	-0.2263
Unemployment rate	-0.0003	-0.0003	-0.0003	-0.0003	-0.0003
Housing starts	0.0017	0.0017	0.0017	0.0017	0.0024
Real per-capita income	0.0037	0.0064	0.0081	0.0110	0.0222
Businesses	0.0046	0.0049	0.0052	0.0064	0.0175

[a]This risk measure is discussed in Section VI.B.3.

Table 9

Fixed-Effect Estimate of the Impact of Deposit Interest Rates on Bank Riskness[d]

Dependent Variable: Bank loan portfolio risk, measured by pseudo-beta[a]

Independent Variable	Equation 1	Equation 2
Average interest rate paid on deposits	-1.4127[c] (0.4230)	-4.2743[c] (0.3310)
Capital-to-asset ratio	0.0042[c] (0.0010)	0.0020[c] (0.0010)
Real deposits (in millions)	-0.0974[c] (0.0455)	-0.1991[c] (0.0412)
Average interest rate * deregulation	2.8100[c] (0.3740)	3.5196[c] (0.3604)
U.S. Treasury bill rate	1.6878[c] (0.2823)	2.3399[c] (0.2711)
Unemployment	-0.0175[c] (0.0011)	
Housing starts	0.0516[c] (0.0046)	
Real per-capita income	0.0001 (0.0056)	
Businesses	-0.0300[c] (0.0060)	
Number of observations	3502	4278
Adjusted R-squared	0.1986	0.0535

[a]Pseudo-beta is defined in Section VI.B.1.
[b]Standard errors are in parentheses below coefficients.
[c]Coefficient is significantly different from zero at the five-percent level.
[d]All variables are in terms of deviations from the individual bank mean; see Section VII.C for the explanation.

Table 10

Fixed-Effect Estimate of the Impact of Deposit Interest Rates on Bank Riskiness[d]

Dependent Variable: Bank loan portfolio risk, measured by pseudo-variance[a]

Independent Variable	Equation 1	Equation 2
Average interest rate paid on deposits	-0.1044[c] (0.0375)	-0.5562[c] (0.0271)
Capital-to-asset ratio	0.0001 (0.0001)	-0.0004[c] (0.0001)
Real deposits (in millions)	-0.0030 (0.0040)	-0.0079[c] (0.0034)
Average interest rate * deregulation	0.0222 (0.0332)	0.2623[c] (0.0295)
U.S. Treasury bill rate	0.1018[c] (0.0251)	0.1087[c] (0.0222)
Unemployment	-0.0007[c] (0.0001)	
Housing starts	-0.0015[c] (0.0004)	
Real per-capita income	-0.0052[c] (0.0005)	
Businesses	-0.0036[c] (0.0005)	
Number of observations	3502	4278
Adjusted R-squared	0.1771	0.1533

[a]Pseudo-variance is defined in section VI.B.2.
[b]Standard errors are in parentheses below coefficients.
[c]Coefficient is significantly different from zero at the five-percent level.
[d]All variables are in terms of deviations from the individual bank mean; see Section VII.C for the explanation.

Table 11

Estimate of the Simultaneous Model
of Deposit Interest Rates and Bank Riskiness

Dependent Variables: Equation (1), bank loan portfolio risk, measured by pseudo-beta[a]; equation (4), average deposit interest rates

Independent Variable	Equation 1	Equation 4
Intercept	0.5479[c] (0.0391)[b]	0.0360[c] (0.0070)
Average interest rate paid on deposits	10.4337[c] (1.3368)	
Bank riskiness (pseudo-beta)		-0.0072 (0.0079)
Capital-to-asset ratio	0.0188[c] (0.0015)	-0.0012[c] (0.0001)
Real deposits (in millions)	0.1692[c] (0.0173)	
Deregulation	-0.7104[c] (0.0423)	0.0469[c] (0.0041)
Average interest rate * deregulation	6.2608[c] (0.8247)	
Bank riskiness (pseudo-beta) * deregulation		-0.0313[c] (0.0048)
U.S. Treasury bill rate	-4.1729[c] (0.6035)	-0.1442[c] (0.0483)
Unemployment	-0.0087[c] (0.0013)	-0.0001 (0.0001)
Housing starts	0.0194[c] (0.0036)	0.0003 (0.0002)
Real per-capita income	0.0057 (0.0032)	-0.0004[c] (0.0002)

Businesses	0.0077[c]	-0.0003[c]
	(0.0018)	(0.0001)
Secondary-market CD rate		0.3970[c]
		(0.0345)
Number of observations	3501	3501

[a]Pseudo-beta is defined in Section VI.B.1.
[b]Standard errors are in parentheses below coefficients.
[c]Coefficient is significantly different from zero at the five-percent level.

Table 12

Estimate of the Simultaneous Model
of Deposit Interest Rates and Bank Riskiness

Dependent Variables: For equation (1), bank loan portfolio risk, measured by pseudo-variance[a]; for equation (4), average deposit interest rates

Independent Variable	*Equation 1*	*Equation 4*
Intercept	0.0557[c] (0.0032)[b]	-0.0052 (0.0089)
Average interest rate paid on deposits	-1.5539[c] (0.1085)	
Bank riskiness (pseudo-variance)		1.0763[c] (0.3271)
Capital-to-asset ratio	-0.0010[c] (0.0001)	-0.0012[c] (0.0001)
Real deposits (in millions)	-0.0064[c] (0.0014)	
Deregulation	-0.0419[c] (0.0034)	0.0324[c] (0.0044)
Average interest rate * deregulation	0.9508[c] (0.0669)	
Bank riskiness (pseudo-variance) * deregulation		0.1667 (0.1647)
U.S. Treasury bill rate	0.5532[c] (0.0490)	-0.2174[c] (0.0717)
Unemployment	0.0001 (0.0001)	-0.0009[c] (0.0002)
Housing starts	-0.0007[c] (0.0003)	0.0002 (0.0002)
Real per-capita income	-0.0006[c] (0.0003)	0.0012[c] (0.0004)

Businesses	0.0001	-0.0010[c]
	(0.0001)	(0.0001)
Secondary-market CD rate		0.4037[c]
		(0.0410)
Number of observations	3501	3501

[a]Pseudo-variance is defined in section VI.B.2.
[b]Standard errors are in parentheses below coefficients.
[c]The coefficient is significant at the five-percent level.

VIII. Empirical Evidence on Bank Failures

This chapter considers the repercussions of deregulation on bank risk, and the consequences of this altered risk-interest rate relationship for bank failures. It offers a two-stage model that allows deregulation to affect bank portfolio risk, which in turn affects the probability of bank failure. This failure model differs from the primary empirical model of Chapter VII by distinguishing between systematic risk, captured by pseudo-beta, and the total probability of bank failure, denoted by the discrete-outcome variable bank status. The first section of this chapter specifies the recursive model; the second section estimates the model, and explores the economic significance of the estimates.

Additionally, this chapter provides supplementary information on the connection between deregulation and the nature of the banks that failed. (Simple means for the failed and non-failed banks are presented in Chapter VII.) Since deregulation allowed greater competition in the banking industry than before, many new banks entered the industry. The final section of this chapter, then, reports simple summary statistics that illuminate key characteristics of these new entrants in terms of their failure or survival.

A. A Recursive Failure Model

1. The Empirical Specification

Banks fail for many reasons. One possibility is that the riskiness of the bank's investments is high; another is that a downturn in local economic conditions weakens the bank; still other explanations include fraud, poor management technique, and competition from other financial intermediaries. The model developed here aspires to illuminate any role of deregulation in bank failures by differentiating between bank portfolio riskiness (and the changes in riskiness evoked by deregulation) and the state of the local economy.

Fundamentally, the model proposes that the institutional changes encompassed by deregulation alter the incentives facing banks in portfolio-risk decisions. Furthermore, the model tests whether this change in bank riskiness caused by deregulation directly affects the ultimate survival or failure of the bank. Both the theoretical model and the primary empirical model describe changes in bank riskiness after deregulation, but the two-stage failure model built here extends this formulation to examine the impact of this regulatory change on the probability of bank failure.

Since this failure model augments the primary model in Chapter VII.B, the first of the two equations in the recursive structure is equation (1) from that chapter. It is repeated here for reference:

$$
\begin{aligned}
(1) \qquad \text{Risk} = {}& a_1 + b_1(\text{interest rate}) + b_2(K/A) \\
& + b_3(\text{deposits}) + b_4(\text{dereg}) \\
& + b_5(\text{dereg*interest rate}) + b_6(\text{t-bill}) \\
& + b_7(\text{unemployment}) + b_8(\text{houses}) \\
& + b_9(\text{income}) + b_{10}(\text{businesses}) + e
\end{aligned}
$$

Again, this specification allows deregulation of deposit interest rates to change the portfolio risk-interest rate relationship; it is through this channel that deregulation affects portfolio riskiness.

In the second equation, the model turns to the probability of bank failure. First, it specifies the interconnection among deregulation, portfolio risk, and the probability of bank failure: Bank failures depend upon portfolio riskiness, measured by pseudo-beta, and portfolio riskiness depends on interest-rate deregulation, as estimated by equation (1). To assess the impact of the local economy on bank failures, which is one of the aims of this model, the second equation also includes as explanatory variables the economic factors utilized in the previous chapters: the unemployment rate, real per-capita personal income, the number of housing starts, and the number of business establishments. Bank failure also depends on the financial resources that the bank can draw upon in troubled times; this "cushion" is proxied by the capital-to-asset ratio. Finally, the size of the bank may affect its eventual survival or failure, so total deposits are included to control for bank size. Thus, the second equation of the failure model is this:

(5) $$\text{Status} = a_2 + b_{11}(\text{risk}) + b_{12}(\text{K/A})$$
$$+ b_{13}(\text{deposits}) + b_{14}(\text{unemployment})$$
$$+ b_{15}(\text{income}) + b_{16}(\text{houses})$$
$$+ b_{17}(\text{businesses}) + e$$

where status represents the eventual outcome of the bank, failure or survival (defined in Section VI.B.3), and the other variables are defined as in the earlier regression. Risk in equation (5) consists of the estimated value of risk from equation (1); this makes the model recursive in structure. As well, it is through this relationship that institutional changes evoked by deregulation affect bank failure in this model. Equations (1) and (5), then, comprise the bank failure model.

2. Empirical Estimate of the Recursive Failure Model

This section turns to the results from estimating the two-stage failure model, consisting of equations (1) and (5). The model's recursive nature indicates that OLS can be used to estimate the equations individually. Since equation (5) is a discrete-outcome model, it is more appropriately estimated with a maximum likelihood technique, so a probit model is employed. Pseudo-beta serves as the risk measure in equation (1); it is chosen because this failure model distinguishes between portfolio risk, or systematic risk, in equation (1), and the total probability of bank failure in equation (5).

Table 13 reports the OLS estimates of the model specified by equation (1), using pseudo-beta as the risk measure, and equation (5). The estimate of equation (1), shown in the first column, is, of course, the same as that shown in Table 5. To summarize, the coefficient on deposit interest rates produces a negative effect on portfolio riskiness before deregulation, but has a strong and positive impact on riskiness after deregulation. The estimated values of risk from this model are used in the regression of equation (5); the resulting coefficients are displayed in the second column of Table 13. The results show that the coefficient for estimated risk is positively related to bank failure; its standard error, however, is relatively large. The capital-to-asset ratio coefficient holds the expected negative relationship with bank failure, and is statistically significant. The coefficient on total bank deposits, the proxy for bank size, also exhibits the expected negative sign. Since bank status takes on the value of one only if it is closed by the federal government, this negative relationship denotes the government policy that some banks are "too big" to fail.

Finally, the macroeconomic variable coefficients display conflicting patterns of influence on bank failures. The coefficients on unemployment and housing starts imply that a downturn in the economy leads to an increased probability of bank failure, whereas the coefficients on per-capita income and the number of businesses suggest that an economic downturn elicits a smaller probability of failure. The conflicting implications probably occur because each economic variable reflects the state of the economy with differing lags in time. The likelihood ratio test of the combined influence of the macroeconomic variables rejects the null hypothesis that their coefficients jointly equal zero.[1]

Since equation (5) is estimated using the probit method, the coefficients do not correspond directly to partial derivatives, as in an OLS regression. Table 14 computes the estimated change in the probability of failure with respect to the explanatory variable coefficients at several points. The move from the first-quartile value to the third-quartile value of estimated value of risk corresponds to a 1.3 percent rise in the probability of failure; the change from first to fourth quartile values creates a six percent increase in the probability of failure. The capital-to-asset ratio, though statistically significant, has a weaker economic impact on the probability of failure: the first- to third-quartile change prompts a one-half percent decrease in the probability of failure. The coefficient on deposit size produces a 0.1 percent decrease in the dependent variable for the interquartile range. The interquartile ranges of the macroeconomic variables display different estimates of the importance of the state of the local economy in explaining bank failures: The unemployment coefficient implies a two percent increase in bank-failure probability; real per-capita personal income, a one percent increase; the number of businesses, a 0.1 percent increase; and housing starts, a 0.04 decline.

The fitted values of this failure model summarize the impact of deregulation on bank failure, through its influence on portfolio riskiness, so the estimated model can be used in simulations. Specifically, consider the following counterfactual: What would be the impact of a change in deposit interest rates on the probability of bank failure, if deregulation had not altered the interest rate-risk relationship? In contrast, how does the significance of the impact of interest rate movements on bank failures change under deregulation?

Assume the usual interquartile rise in deposit interest rates. Then, using the partial derivative of estimated risk at its median value, computations show that this change in interest rates ultimately evokes a 0.21 percent decrease in the probability of bank failure under regulation of deposit interest rates. In contrast, the same fluctuation in interest rates, assuming that deregulation has occurred, induces a 0.33 percent increase in the probability of bank failure. Of course, if this change is computed using the partial derivative at the maximum level of estimated risk, the difference grows: Without deregulation, the interest rate alteration decreases the probability of failure by 0.37 percent; with deregulation, by 0.6 percent. If instead the original increase in the deposit interest rate moves from the first quartile value to the fourth quartile value, under deregulation the ultimate impact becomes a 0.8 percent increase in the probability of bank failure; using the partial derivative of risk at its fourth quartile value magnifies this estimate to a one-and-one-half percent increase in the probability of bank failure. These estimates suggest that deposit-rate deregulation affected bank failures in an economically significant way.

The two-stage failure model, then, indicates that the deregulation of deposit interest rates had an economically significant impact on the probability of bank failure. Deregulation changed the statistical and economic significance of the influence of interest rates on risk, which in turn affected the probability of bank failure. Macroeconomic forces also help to explain bank failures, but the impact of deregulation on bank failures remains economically important.

B. Evidence on New Entrants

Deregulation of financial intermediaries encouraged entry into banking. This section examines some evidence on the role of new entrants in the banking crisis that followed deregulation. New entrants are defined as banks that appear in the data set for the first time after 1980.

Due to the newly-relaxed regulatory structure, new entrants

may be attracted to the industry because of the new opportunities to engage in additional risk-taking; investors interested in riskier activities now have new opportunities to participate in these riskier projects. This, in turn, might lead to more bank failures within the group of new entrants. Also, the new entrants might be expected to more aggressively compete for deposits, the necessary base for additional investment activity. With deregulation, competition for deposits would occur through differential deposit rates paid by individual banks, so new entrants might display higher average deposit interest rates, if indeed they pursue rapid-growth strategies.

Table 15 addresses the primary differences in characteristics between new entrants and established banks; it summarizes averages of the main explanatory variables for these two groups. Most surprising, perhaps, is the fact that new entrants, on average, hold lower-risk portfolios than already-established banks. (The difference is statistically significant.) Similarly, the averages show that new entrants do not, on average, attempt to compete more aggressively for deposits by offering higher deposit interest rates; on the contrary, average deposit rates are lower for new entrants. This difference, however, is not statistically significant. New entrants generally exhibit a higher capital-to-asset ratio than established firms; this fact arises because of the time it takes to build an investment (asset) portfolio. New entrants also tend to be smaller than established banks.

Table 16 sheds light on the role of new entrants in bank failures in the 1980's; it summarizes the number and percent of bank failures by groups, new entrants and established banks. Of the banks that fail in the sample, approximately thirty percent are new entrants, so new entrants do not constitute the majority of failures. New entrants do, however, suffer proportionately more failures; about five percent of all new entrants eventually fail, while less than two percent of the group of established banks fail during the sample period. The chi-squared statistic analyzes the null hypothesis that the frequency of bank failure does not depend on a bank's classification as an established firm or a new entrant. The alternative hypothesis is that bank failure is related to the bank's new-entry status. The test statistic for this table equals 13.44, so the test rejects the null hypothesis; bank failure is related to the bank's status as a new entrant.

New entrants to banking, then, do not on average show higher portfolio risk or higher average deposit interest rates. However, they do exhibit a greater tendency to fail than established banks. New-entrant status plays a role in the banking crisis of the 1980's, but it is not the only factor involved in an explanation of the crisis, as the previous chapter of empirical tests demonstrates.

Notes

1. The computed LR statistic is 255.99.

Table 13

Estimate of the Impact of Interest-Rate Deregulation
on Bank Failures

Dependent Variable: For equation (1), bank loan portfolio risk, measured by pseudo-beta; for equation (5), bank status[a]

Independent Variable	Equation 1	Equation 5
Intercept	0.7828[c] (0.0341)[b]	-5.0649[c] (0.7032)
Average interest rate paid on deposits	-1.8281[c] (0.5171)	
Capital-to-asset ratio	0.0019[c] (0.0009)	-0.0289[c] (0.0072)
Real deposits (in millions)	0.1302[c] (0.0177)	-2.0316[c] (0.3461)
Deregulation	-0.3607[c] (0.0311)	
Average interest rate * deregulation	4.6730[c] (0.5522)	
Unemployment	-0.0087[c] (0.0013)	0.0877[c] (0.0137)
Housing starts	0.0270[c] (0.0038)	-0.0619 (0.0368)
Real per-capita income	-0.0001 (0.0033)	0.2763[c] (0.0283)
Businesses	-0.0002 (0.0018)	0.0364[c] (0.0139)
Portfolio Riskiness (estimated pseudo-beta)		0.7931 (0.6160)

Number of observations	3501	3502
Adjusted R-squared (1) or Likelihood Ratio statistic (5)	0.1980	286.9[c]

[a]Pseudo-beta is defined in Section VI.B.1, while bank status is defined in Section VI.B.3.
[b]Standard errors are in parentheses below coefficients.
[c]Coefficient is significantly different from zero at the five-percent level.

Table 14

Estimates of the Partial Derivatives
of Explanatory Variables on Bank Failures

Dependent Variable: Bank status, equal to one if the bank fails in the sample period, and zero otherwise[a]

Independent Variable	Q0	Q1	Q2	Q3	Q4
Estimated risk	0.0261	0.0354	0.0408	0.0443	0.0715
Capital-to-asset ratio	-0.0011	-0.0004	-0.0004	-0.0003	0.0
Real deposits	-0.0329	-0.0291	-0.0268	-0.0230	0.0
Unemploy-ment rate	0.0003	0.0007	0.0012	0.0021	0.0274
Per-capita income	0.0002	0.0016	0.0036	0.0108	0.0748
Housing starts	-0.0008	-0.0008	-0.0008	-0.0008	-0.0002
Businesses	0.0004	0.0004	0.0005	0.0005	0.0011

[a]The definition of this risk measure is discussed in Section VI.B.3.

Table 15

Selected Averages for Louisiana Banks, by Status as New Entrants

Variable	Established Banks	New-Entry Banks
Bank portfolio risk (pseudo-beta)[a]	0.777 (0.229)[b]	0.664[c] (0.251)
Bank portfolio risk (pseudo-variance)[a]	0.014 (0.018)	0.007 (0.003)[c]
Average interest rate paid on deposits	0.053 (0.019)	0.053 (0.019)
Capital-to-asset ratio	0.089 (0.031)	0.126[c] (0.098)
Real deposits (millions)	0.094 (0.211)	0.066 (0.240)
Unemployment rate	0.010 (0.040)	0.112[c] (0.037)
Businesses established (thousands)	2.203 (3.046)	4.916[c] (4.379)
Real income per-capita (thousands)	8.474 (1.852)	10.084[c] (10.709)
Housing starts (thousands)	0.663 (1.235)	0.881[c] (1.321)

[a]Pseudo-beta and pseudo-variance are defined in sections VI.B.1 and VI.B.2, respectively.
[b]Standard errors are in parentheses below coefficient estimates.
[c]The difference between the means in the two categories is significantly different from zero at the five-percent level.

Table 16

Classification of Established Banks and New Entrants
by Failure and Survival

Frequency Percent Row Percent Column Percent	Established Banks	New-entry Banks	Total
Surving Banks	2115 85.14 87.18 98.10	311 12.52 12.82 94.82	2426 97.67
Failed Banks	41 1.65 70.69 1.90	17 0.68 29.31 5.18	58 2.33
Total	2156 86.80	328 13.20	2484 100.00

Chi-squared test-statistic: 13.44

Note: Section VIII.B explains the definition of new entrants.

IX. Conclusions

This book examines empirical answers to the question, "Did deregulation play a part in the financial distress of the 1980's?" I propose that the locally depressed economy is not the sole factor involved in the financial problems of the area. Instead, the changes in institutional structure due to deregulation must also be considered.

The empirical tests offer evidence that deregulation has changed the magnitude of the influence of deposit interest rates on bank risk choices. While the coefficients describing the relationship between interest rates and risk are negative or insignificantly different from zero in the regulated period, the coefficients are significantly positive in the post-deregulation period. The strongly positive relationship between pseudo-beta and deposit interest rates holds under alternate empirical model specifications that allow for individual bank effects and simultaneity.

Furthermore, the recursive failure model shows that, under deregulation, the impact of the change in the interest rate-risk relationship has an economically significant influence on the probability of bank failure. Deregulation affects bank failures through its influence on bank portfolio risk. Measures of the local economy also hold statistically significant connections to bank failures, but the deregulation effect dominates the local-economy effect in terms of economic significance in this model.

What do these results suggest for bank regulation? As a first step, bank regulators might use deposit interest rates as a method for determining which banks should be more closely watched. Should deposit ceilings be reinstated? Practical considerations cast doubt on the feasibility of returning to the same regulatory and institutional structure of the past. A new type of ceiling might effectively limit bank risk-taking, however; one proposal that deposit ceilings be linked to market rates might be a viable alternative. Finally, the present deposit insurance system needs further scrutiny, since it is through its distortions that the positive link between risk and deposit interest rates occurs.

123

Appendix A: Comparison of Portfolio Risk Choices

This appendix describes the relationship of the chosen portfolio risk Θ'' for a completely debt-financed bank with no deposit insurance, to Θ^* and Θ', the social optimum and the profit maximization choice with deposit insurance, respectively. It demonstrates that $\Theta^* < \Theta'' < \Theta'$. The first proposition establishes the relationship between Θ'' and Θ^*, and the second proposition characterizes the relationship between Θ'' and Θ'.[1]

Proposition A1: Given $(1 + r) < M(\Theta^*)$, a fully debt-financed bank without deposit insurance chooses a portfolio with more risk than the social optimum, or $\Theta'' > \Theta^*$.

Proof: We wish to compare equation (2), which defines the first order condition for Θ^*, with equation (4'), the first order condition for Θ''. The second integral in each equation is the same and each is positive. However, the second integral in equation (2) is a larger positive value than the second integral in equation (4'), since the binding deposit-rate ceiling in (2) implies that $(1 + r)$ is smaller in equation (2). As before, the concavity of the bank objective function with respect to Θ implies that Θ'' defined in (4') must be greater than Θ^* defined in (2), since the former is a smaller positive number at the optimum. ◄

Proposition A2: Given $(1 + r) < M(\Theta^*)$, a fully debt-financed bank chooses a portfolio with more risk when deposit insurance is present than when it is not; that is, $\Theta' > \Theta''$.

Proof: The proof is similar to the proof of Proposition 1 in Chapter V. The first order condition (4') for a bank without deposit insurance

125

differs from the first order condition (4) for a bank with full deposit insurance by only the first term. Since this first term in (4') is negative, the second term in (4') is positive. Again, the concavity of the bank objective function with respect to Θ implies that Θ' defined in (4) must therefore be greater than Θ'' defined in (4'). ◄

The ordering of the different risk levels, then, is $\Theta^* < \Theta'' < \Theta'$; the socially optimal risk level is less than the debt-financed bank's choice with or without deposit insurance, but the bank's risk choice without deposit insurance is less than the choice with deposit insurance.

Notes

1. All numbered equations are identified by the same number used in Chapter V.

Appendix B: Data Sources

A. Call Report Data

The data for each bank's loans, deposits, interest expenses, non-performing loans, capital-to-asset ratio, and net-income-to-assets ratios were collected from the Statement of Condition and Income filed by each bank annually. The data set consists of all banks in Louisiana that filed at least one such report during the years 1974-89.

The total loan amount is divided into several categories, depending on the use of the loan. These categories are listed in Table A1. Not all categories are reported each year. For a single bank, the amount of loans in a given category divided by total loans gives the weight of that category in the portfolio; this weight is used in calculating the pseudo-beta. The equity-market proxy used for each loan category in these calculations is discussed below.

Variables related to a bank's deposits are total deposits and interest expenses on deposits. Annual total deposits are deflated with the GNP deflator to obtain total real deposits. These total real deposits are reported in units of millions in the regressions. The average interest rate paid on deposits each year by each bank is calculated by dividing total (nominal) interest expenses by total (nominal) bank deposits.

The weighted average of U.S. Treasury bills that serves as a proxy for bank risk-constant asset returns is computed using average reported proportions of loans in several maturity groups. Banks report the proportion of loans that are re-negotiable in three categories: those re-negotiable after one year, after five years, and after more than five years. Since banks have only recently begun reporting this information, it is not available for my sample; instead, the 1990 figures provide a benchmark for calculating a representative weight for each category for each year in the sample. In 1990, the weights for the categories are sixty-five percent for loans re-negotiable after one year; twenty-five percent, after five years; and ten percent, after more than five years. For year t, the corresponding Treasury bill rates are the year t rate, the year t - 5 rate, and the year t - 10 year rate. The proxy for bank portfolio returns, m(Θ) in year t, is then

$$m(\Theta) = 0.65*r_t + 0.25*r_{t-5} + 0.10*r_{t-10}.$$

This is the proxy whose coefficient estimate is reported in the tables as the U.S. Treasury bill rate.

B. Data Used in Calculation of Risk Measures

A pseudo-beta and a pseudo-variance risk measure are constructed for each bank for each year. For most loan categories, a stock-market proxy is found, and the estimated beta for that industry is calculated from the daily returns for each year. The data on the industry's stock-market returns come from the Center for the Research of Security Prices (CRSP) data tapes. For Government National Mortgage Association (GNMA) returns, the monthly returns were taken from issues of the *Federal Reserve Bulletin*. The proxy for each loan category is listed in Table A1. The pseudo-beta for a bank is the weighted sum of the individual loan category betas, where the weight used is the bank's portfolio weight described above. The pseudo-variance is the weighted sum of the variance-covariance matrix of the loan category proxies, the market returns.

The probability-of-failure risk measure assigns to each bank a status of one if it fails at some time during the sample, and a status of zero if it survives the sample period. Banks are classified as failed in the year in which the FDIC reported them as failed. A list of failed banks is published by the FDIC in each *Annual Report*.

C. Other Data

Historical data of the number of bank failures for Figures 1 and 2, as well as Table 1, come from various editions of the FDIC *Annual*

Report. The annual number of insured banks comes from the *Statistical Abstract of the U.S., Colonial Times to 1970*, and the *Statistical Abstract of the U.S.* for years after 1970.

Data for Figures 5 through 7 come from their respective agency annual reports. For Figure 5, the information is procured from various editions of *The Annual Report* of the Board of Governors of the Federal Reserve System; for Figures 6 and 7, the material is from *The Annual Report* of the FDIC.

The data comprising the figures in Chapter III, also utilized as the proxies for the condition of the local economy in the regressions, come from the several sources. The unemployment data are reported by the U.S. Bureau of Labor Statistics; these annual parish-level data are averages of monthly parish-level amounts. The per-capita personal income data come from the U.S. Department of Commerce "Local Area Personal Income" reports. "County Business Patterns" from the U.S. Bureau of the Census provides the number of business establishments. Finally, the number of housing starts is also collected by the Bureau of the Census, and reported in "Construction Reports: Housing Units Authorized by Building Permits and Public Contracts."

Table A1

Loan Categories Reported to the Federal Reserve and
Industry Proxies for Pseudo-Beta Calculation

Construction and land development loans, secured by real estate
Proxy: Real estate development corporations

Farm loans, secured by real estate
Proxy: Agricultural production firms

Residential loans, FHA/VA, secured by real estate
Proxy: Government National Mortgage Association (GNMA) secondary-
market bond returns

1-4 family conventional residential loans, secured by real estate
Proxy: GNMA secondary-market bond returns

5+ family conventional residential loans, secured by real estate
Proxy: GNMA secondary-market bond returns

Non-farm, non-residential loans, secured by real estate
Proxy: General contractors of industrial buildings and warehouses

Municipal obligations
Proxy: Returns on Moody's Bond Buyer government bond series

Loans to financial institutions
Proxy: Federal funds interest rate

Securities loans
Proxy: Security brokerages

Agricultural production loans
Proxy: Agricultural products

Commercial and industrial loans
Proxy: Crude oil and related products

Loans to individuals, including auto, credit cards, and installment
Proxy: Personal credit corporations

Bankers' Acceptances
Proxy: 90-day prime bankers' acceptance rate

Lease financing
Proxy: Leasing business credit institutions

All other loans
Proxy: Equal-weighted average of other proxies

References

Allen, Paul and William Wilhelm. 1988. "The Impact of the 1980 Depository Institutions Deregulation and Monetary Control Act on Market Value and Risk." *Journal of Money, Credit, and Banking* 20: 364-80.

Avery, Robert and Gerald Hanweck. 1984. "A Dynamic Analysis of Bank Failures." In *Bank Structure and Competition*. Chicago: Federal Reserve Bank of Chicago Symposium Proceedings.

Boyd, John and Stanley Graham. 1986. "Risk, Regulation, and Bank Holding Company Expansion into Nonbanking." *Federal Reserve Bank of Minneapolis Quarterly Review* (Spring) 2-17.

Cornett, Marcia and Hassan Tehranian. 1990. "An Examination of the Impact of the Garn-St. Germain Depository Institutions Act of 1982 on Commercial Banks and Savings and Loans." *Journal of Finance* 45: 95-111.

Diamond, Douglas, and Philip Dybvig. 1983. "Bank Runs, Deposit Insurance, and Liquidity." *Journal of Political Economy* 91: 401-419.

------ 1986. "Banking Theory, Deposit Insurance, and Bank Regulation." *Journal of Business* 59:55-68.

Dothan, Uri and Joseph Williams. 1980. "Banks, Bankruptcy, and Public Regulation." *Journal of Banking and Finance* 4: 65-87.

Eisenbeis, Robert. 1986. "Regulatory Policies and Financial Stability." In *Debt, Financial Stability, and Public Policy*. Kansas City: Federal Reserve Bank of Kansas City Symposium Proceedings.

Federal Deposit Insurance Corporation. *Annual Report*. Washington, D.C.: Federal Deposit Insurance Corporation.

Federal Reserve System Board of Governors. *Annual Report*.

Friedman, Milton. 1960. *A Program for Monetary Stability.* New York: Fordham University Press.

Gunther, Jeffery. 1989. "Texas Banking Conditions: Managerial versus Economic Factors." *Federal Reserve Bank of Dallas Financial Industry Studies* (October) 1-18.

Heymann, Daniel and Axel Leijonhufvud. 1989. *1989 Ryde Lectures: High Inflations.* Manuscript.

Hsiao, Cheng. 1986. *Analysis of Panel Data.* Cambridge: The Cambridge University Press.

Kane, Edward. 1985. *The Gathering Crisis in Federal Deposit Insurance.* Cambridge, MA: The MIT Press.

Kareken, John. 1981. "Deregulating Commercial Banks: The Watchword Should Be Caution." *Federal Reserve Bank of Minneapolis Quarterly Review* (Spring-Summer) 1-5.

------ 1983. "The First Step in Bank Deregulation: What about the FDIC?" *American Economic Review* 73: 198-203.

Kareken, John, and Neil Wallace. 1978. "Deposit Insurance and Bank Regulation: A Partial Equilibrium Exposition." *Journal of Business* 51: 413-438.

Kindleberger, Charles. 1989. *Manias, Panics, and Crashes: A History of Financial Crises.* New York: Basic Books.

Klein, Benjamin. 1974. "Competitive Interest Payments on Bank Deposits and the Long-Run Demand for Money." *American Economic Review* 64: 931-961.

Minsky, Hyman. 1977. "A Theory of Systematic Fragility." In *Financial Crises: Institutions and Markets in a Fragile Environment.* Ed. Edward Altman and Arnold Sametz.

O'Driscoll, Gerald. 1988. "Bank Failures: The Deposit Insurance

Connection." *Contemporary Policy Issues* April, 1988.

Pantalone, Coleen and Marjorie Platt. 1987. "Predicting Commercial Bank Failure since Deregulation." *New England Economic Review* (July/August) 37-47.

Rolnick, Arthur. 1987. "The Benefits of Bank Deposit Rate Ceilings: New Evidence on Bank Rates and Risk in the 1920's." *Federal Reserve Bank of Minneapolis Quarterly Review* (Summer) 2-18.

Schaefer, Stephen. 1987. "The Design of Bank Regulation and Supervision: Some Lessons from the Theory of Finance." In *Threats to International Stability*. Ed. Richard Portes.

Short, Genie and Jeffery Gunther. 1988. "The Texas Thrift Situation: Implications for the Texas Financial Industry." *Federal Reserve Bank of Dallas Financial Industry Studies* (September) 1-11.

Smirlock, Michael. 1984. "An Analysis of Bank Risk and Deposit Rate Ceilings: Evidence from the Capital Markets." *Journal of Monetary Economics* 13: 195-210.

Smith, Bruce. 1984. "Private Information, Deposit Interest Rates, and the 'Stability' of the Banking System." *Journal of Monetary Economics* 14: 293-317.

U.S. Comptroller of the Currency. 1988. *Bank Failure: An Evaluation of the Factors Contributing to the Failure of National Banks.*

U.S. Department of Commerce. Bureau of the Census. *Housing Units Authorized by Building Permits and Public Contracts.* Construction Reports C40. Washington, D.C.: Government Printing Office.

------ *County Business Patterns.* Washington, D.C.: Government Printing Office.

U.S. Department of Commerce. Bureau of Economic Analysis. *Local*

Area Personal Income. Washington, D.C.: Government
Printing Office.

Wall, Larry. 1987. "Has Bank Holding Companies' Diversification
Affected Their Risk of Failure?" *Journal of Economics and
Business* 39: 313-26.

Wallace, Neil. 1988. "Another Attempt to Explain an Illiquid Banking
System." *Federal Reserve Bank of Minneapolis Quarterly
Review* (Fall) 3-16.

White, Halbert. 1980. "A Heteroskedasticity-Consistent Covariance
Matrix Estimator and a Direct Test for Heteroskedasticity."
Econometrica 48: 817-838.

White, Lawrence. 1984. *Free Banking in Britain: Theory, Experience,
and Debate, 1800-1845.* Cambridge: Oxford University Press.

Williamson, Stephen. 1988. "Liquidity, Banking, and Bank Failures."
International Economic Review 29: 25-43.

Wooldridge, Jeffery. "A Computationally Simple Heteroskedasticity and
Serial Correlation Robust Standard Error for the Linear
Regression Model." *Economics Letters* 31: 239-43.

Index

Non-performing loans
  described 54
O'Driscoll, Gerald 9
Oil industry 21
Oil prices 22
Pantalone, Coleen 41, 42
Personal income
  data sources 131
  empirical model and 71
  estimates in bank failure model 112
  estimates in bank status model 79
  estimates in pseudo-beta model 74
  estimates in pseudo-variance model 77
  figures of 23
Platt, Marjorie 41, 42
Pseudo-beta
  data sources 130
  estimated impact of deposit interest rates on 73, 84
  estimates in bank failure model 112
  figures of 55, 56
  formula 55
  in bank failure model 111
  model estimated with 73, 84
  reasons for 55
  stock-market proxies 130

Pseudo-variance
  data sources 130
  estimated impact of deposit interest rates on 76, 86
  figures of 57
  formula 57
  model estimated with 76, 86
  reasons for 57
  stock-market proxies 130
Recursive model 109
Regulated period
  compared to unregulated period 69
Risk
  Theoretical definition 46
Risk-constant asset returns
  defined 129
  empirical model and 71
  estimates in bank status model 79
  estimates in pseudo-beta model 74
  estimates in pseudo-variance model 77
  in data set 59
  nominal or real 59
Rolnick, Arthur 40, 42
Short, Genie 41
Simulation of bank failure model 112
Simulations
  of bank status model 79
  of pseudo-beta model 76, 84
  of pseudo-variance model 77